Making the Mathematics CURRICULUM Count

A Guide for Middle
and High School
Principals

NATIONAL ASSOCIATION
OF SECONDARY SCHOOL
PRINCIPALS

Reston, VA

With generous support from

MINNESOTA LIFE

St. Paul, MN

NATIONAL ASSOCIATION
of SECONDARY SCHOOL
PRINCIPALS

1904 Association Drive
Reston, VA 20191-1537
www.principals.org

Barry Stark, *President*
Larry D. Bradley, *President-Elect*
Gerald N. Tirozzi, *Executive Director*
Lenor G. Hersey, *Deputy Executive Director*
Robert N. Farrace, *Director of Publications*
John R. Nori, *Director of Instructional Leadership Resources*
Jeanne Leonard, *Director of Marketing and Sales*
Tanya S. Burke, *Associate Director for Graphics Services*
Judith Richardson, *Principal Author*
Dianne Mero, *Author*
Lisa Schnabel, *Graphic Designer*
Lauren Hillman Taylor, *Proofreader*

ISBN 978-0-88210-374-7

Contents

List of Appendices

Preface

Schools and school districts are under mounting pressure to "make the mathematics curriculum count." As the nation continues moving toward instruction and learning for all students, the stakes are increasing. The pressure mounts with increased requirements of the No Child Left Behind Act, which mandates that demonstrated school improvement must not only be made in the area of reading but now in the area of mathematics.

Making the Mathematics Curriculum Count provides principals with a guide to invest themselves in all aspects of planning, implementing, and monitoring a schoolwide numeracy program. It addresses student mathematics mastery in a whole-school approach that details forming leadership teams; developing a Numeracy Improvement Plan; building instructional capacity in the school; collecting and interpreting local school formative and summative data; implementing increased rigor in the content classrooms; integrating mathematics skills, technology, and problem solving into all content areas; increasing opportunities for equity of participation in mathematics; and encouraging students to be self-directed and to set strong mathematics goals. If schools are to become centers for learning, they must be data driven, student focused, and able to make connections between what students are learning and what they will need in life to become successful. This guide will connect the dots for principals and administrators across the country who are striving to change the culture of numeracy in their schools.

NASSP continues to be at the forefront of secondary school reform. *Making the Mathematics Curriculum Count* is the fourth in the continuing *Breaking Ranks* series that provides resources to principals to enhance their instructional leadership skills and support systemic school improvement.

NASSP continues to seek partnerships and leverage resources to give sustained, high-quality support to principals who lead the charge daily to provide equity of participation to every student in their schools.

Making the Mathematics Curriculum Count details school profiles; valuable leadership strategies for schoolwide improvement, particularly in mathematics and reading; and a series of templates and tools that will help you lead an effective numeracy journey for every student in your school. As principal, you make decisions every day that affect the lives of young people. There is no more important decision that will make more students successful in life than increasing their participation in challenging mathematics classes.

Gerald N. Tirozzi
Executive Director, NASSP

Acknowledgements

This valuable addition to the principals' toolbox, *Making the Mathematics Curriculum Count: A Guide for Middle and High School Principals*, would not exist without the foresight of the executive director of the National Association of Secondary Principals, Dr. Gerald N. Tirozzi. Dr. Tirozzi's vision of making available to principals a mathematics-focused companion piece to *Creating a Culture of Literacy: A Guide for Middle and High School Principals* (NASSP, 2005), in the popular *Breaking Ranks*® series has been realized with the publication of this manual. NASSP is deeply grateful for the generous support of Minnesota Life, making the wide distribution of this manual possible. Serving as principal author, Judith Richardson is the associate director for school improvement at NASSP. Judith is a lifelong mathematics educator, a former principal, a mathematics professor, and an author who initiated an award-winning secondary pre-engineering public-private partnership. Dianne Mero, former principal, NASSP consultant, and coauthor of the Breakthrough High Schools articles featured in *Principal Leadership* magazine, also made outstanding contributions to this manual.

Thank you to the following principals and their staff members for sharing their school profiles through "Notes from the Field," providing many real-school examples of successful mathematics reform efforts:

- Lorine Burrell, Lake Highlands Junior High School, Richardson, TX
- Kay Enright, Georgia O'Keeffe Middle School, Madison, WI
- Robert Hatcher, Campbell Middle School, Houston, TX
- Diane Lauer, Conrad Ball Middle School, Loveland, CO
- Gary Rosenthal, Woodbridge High School, Bridgefield, DE
- Greg Spradling, Durango High School, Durango, CO
- Leslie Standerfer, Melanie Mock, and T. J. Peacher, Estrella Foothills High School, Goodyear, AZ.

Thank you to the contributing principals and schools who provided the rich background material found in practical applications and program descriptions throughout this publication, including Keith Richardson, principal of Arroyo High School (El Monte, CA) and Patrick Delmore, former principal of Georgia O'Keeffe Middle School (Madison, WI).

Foreword

As a provider of life insurance protection, Minnesota Life has proudly served the members of the National Association of Secondary School Principals (NASSP) for more than 73 years. The values we have nurtured since our company was established mirror in many ways the values that leaders like you exhibit every day in your schools: trust, strength, integrity, quality, respect, and community. We are, therefore, very pleased to collaborate with NASSP to support the wide distribution of *Making the Mathematics Curriculum Count: A Guide for Middle and High School Principals*. At a time of increased urgency around science and math student performance and the crucial role of increased mathematics rigor in improving the quality of life for all our young people, this publication provides you with an essential tool to enhance your leadership role. At Minnesota Life, we know the value of financial literacy and the value of leadership. We hope this resource will serve you well.

Minnesota Life Insurance Company

Introduction
Leadership for Numeracy

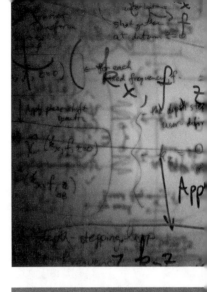

*To become the instructional leader of my school, I must narrow
my scope and maintain my focus.... I recognize that any improvement
of instruction must occur at the classroom level.*

—*Edward Yergalonis*

The principal is called upon again and again to demonstrate wholehearted commitment to school improvement. This is especially true in our current educational and political climate, where accountability pervades any talk of school reform. The entire school community—staff members, parents, students, and district administrators—looks to the principal to display a renewed commitment to promoting the most important facets of education in its school, those that improve learning for all students.

A commitment of this magnitude is not easily defined or accomplished; it takes enormous work and effort when other matters, often important in their own right, clamor for attention. Working through the self-reflection necessary to articulate a realistic and powerful commitment philosophy is often difficult but essential to creating a foundation for change. The philosophy must not only be clearly stated, concisely and simply in your own words, but it must also be modeled in your actions. A personal commitment statement helps keep your instructional focus in mind as you go about your daily tasks.

Adopting a personal commitment statement is not the same as supporting the school's mission statement. In a mission statement, the school community shares an understanding of and a commitment to instructional goals, priorities, assessment procedures, and accountability for the whole school. The principal must decide how to provide the leadership to make that happen each day. A personal commitment statement as simple as "I will devote time each day to improving the numeracy skills of my students" says volumes about your priorities, is easy to remember, and cuts to the heart of the new role you have identified for yourself. Because of what are seen as more urgent matters, a commitment to numeracy has not been voiced as an explicit concern in many schools, yet a large number of our students continue to struggle to find meaning and success in their formal and informal mathematics education and, therefore, jeopardize their future success in the workforce. You are charged with moving this issue to the "front burner" at your school, and there is no more powerful way to accomplish this than by your day-to-day actions in support of your personal commitment to numeracy. Your assertion must be crafted by you, not pressed on you by others; require action on your part, not be focused on what others will do to accomplish your goals; be something you really believe, not a restatement of someone else's vision; and, most important, speak directly to improved instruction and learning in your school. Remember, where you direct your budget, resources, and time will be seen by staff and students as your commitment. "Be sure the commitment you have chosen is one that feels powerful and is likely to yield rich learning and progress" (Wagner and Kegan, 2006, p. 53).

Numeracy?

Mathematics literacy, quantitative literacy, or *numeracy:* for years, mathematics educators have struggled over a designation that embraces both the computational and cognitive skills of the discipline. Regardless of choice of words, most math educators would agree with *New York Times* science reporter Gina Kolata (1997) that:

> Beyond arithmetic and geometry, quantitative literacy also requires logic, data analysis, and probability…. It enables individuals to analyze evidence, to read graphs, to understand logical arguments, to detect logical fallacies, to understand evidence, and to evaluate risks. Quantitative Literacy means knowing *how to reason and how to think* (p. 24).

For the purposes of this manual, we've selected *numeracy*—a contraction of the words *numerical literacy*—as our preferred term. *Numeracy* is a straightforward, one-word designation that intentionally parallels *literacy* for simplicity and ease of use.

Numeracy refers to a set of mathematical and advanced problem-solving skills necessary to succeed in an economy increasingly driven by data. Numeracy means more than the ability to perform mathematical computations. It applies mathematics skills and problem-solving techniques in virtually all areas of life and, therefore, has applications in all content areas.

Once you have made a personal commitment to numeracy, share this vision with stakeholders in a concrete way and follow up immediately with the steps outlined in this manual. Even though the foundation presented in the following chapters—school climate, capacity, collaborative teams, data, rigor, budget, and material and human resources—may be in place, a high level of attention must continue daily. Committing personnel and resources to a schoolwide numeracy program certainly shows your resolve for improving the mathematics achievement of your students. But the best way to effectively motivate your students and teachers is to physically be there with them.

What We Know About Mathematics and What Counts in Schools

■ Numeracy should be seen as a whole-school effort across all content areas.

Literacy is linked to numeracy.

Recently, there has been a much-needed emphasis on literacy in secondary schools. School leaders can seize this opportunity to simultaneously improve students' numeracy skills as well. In March 2006, analysts at ACT studied the test scores of 1.2 million students. Of the 51% of students who were reading on the college level at the time of the test, 94% met the English benchmark and 63% met the mathematics benchmark. Of the 49% not reading on the college level, 41% met the English benchmark and only

16% met the mathematics benchmark. *Students reading on grade level were nearly four times more likely to meet the mathematics benchmark* (ACT, 2006).

If your school is one of the leaders in this area and already has a schoolwide literacy program with a leadership team in place (see *Creating a Culture of Literacy: A Guide for Middle and High School Principals* [NASSP, 2005]), a schoolwide numeracy initiative can be accomplished with the addition of one high-performance team: the numeracy team. This interdisciplinary team is comprised of department and grade-level representatives supported by highly motivated members of the mathematics faculty. The objectives of this team are to collaborate with the literacy initiative and promote the use of problem-solving techniques and activities that use mathematics as a tool across all disciplines. An excellent example is described in "Notes from the Field" at the end of this chapter.

Mathematics achievement relies on increased rigor in the classroom and continual K–12 instruction.

It is crucial that more K–12 educators understand the interdependence of continual successful school instruction and actual mathematics achievement. Students are unlikely to study mathematics or work on mathematics skills outside the classroom; the responsibility for mathematics instruction in the United States rests with the schools. Therefore, the more deliberate the focus of the teachers on rigorous content standards, supported by diversified teaching and intervention strategies, the higher the student achievement.

There are two reasons why principals must ensure that all students are challenged with a rigorous mathematics course each year. First, success in mathematics has been shown to be more school-based than success in reading and "[t]here is clear and compelling evidence that the level of courses students take in high school is one of the best predictors of their success in college and the workplace. This is particularly true in mathematics, where data show a strong correlation between taking higher-level mathematics courses in high school and achieving success in college and employment" (Achieve Inc., 2006, p. 13).

Finally, since most mathematics is school-based, principals must be concerned with retention of mathematics skills over the summer break. In a review of 39 studies, Harris Cooper and his colleagues at Duke University found confirmation of the long-held belief that test scores in mathematics and reading declined over the summer months and that the loss was higher in mathematics than in reading. Cooper explains: "The reason is simple: children's out-of-school environments provide more opportunities for reading than math" (2005, p. 1). In an attempt to address the summer void, principals must ensure that summer programs and school-developed summer learning packets include extensive practice of mathematics skills for all students.

Mathematics assessment scores are improving.

A look at recent research on mathematics achievement confirms that contrary to public perceptions, mathematics scores have steadily increased. The latest results of the National Assessment of Educational Progress (NAEP), commonly referred to as the "Nation's Report Card," validated previous findings that national mathematics scores rose between 2003 and 2005. NAEP achievement levels range from Basic to Proficient to Advanced, each reflecting the level of competency demonstrated over challenging subject matter. Between 1990 and 2005, fourth graders performing at or above Basic increased

■ Principals now have the opportunity to link whole-school literacy with a schoolwide numeracy effort.

■ Mathematics acquisition is the result of school-based learning.

■ Every student must take mathematics classes every year; a K–12 continuum of higher-level mathematics courses results in improved achievement.

■ Summer intervention activities result in more mathematics skills retention.

- Mathematics scores, in general, are on the rise.
- Emphasis on mathematics instruction must begin early and continue throughout schooling.

- Expectations for minority and disadvantaged students must be changed.
- Opportunities for higher-level mathematics courses must be made available for every student with the appropriate support.

- All students need to understand the relationship of mathematics and numeracy to applications in the real world.

by 30 percentage points, and eighth graders at or above Basic increased by 17 percentage points. Fourth graders performing at or above Proficient increased by 23 percentage points, and eighth graders at or above Proficient increased by 15 percentage points. All subgroups improved (Perie, Grigg, and Dion, 2005).

Even looking at student performance internationally, U.S. students are improving. As the Trends in International Mathematics and Science Study shows, U.S. eighth graders improved their mathematics and science scores in 1995, 1999, and 2003 although no other nation educates as diverse a population as does the United States (Farhi, 2007).

To build on this success, it is important to continue to teach and emphasize mathematical skills and thinking in the mathematics classroom and in all other content areas.

The mathematics achievement gap still exists.

As summarized in a 2005 report by the Education Trust, progress on a commitment to close the achievement gaps between income, gender, and ethnic subgroups has been disappointing. "A primary goal of NCLB was to close persistent gaps in achievement. Many states are not achieving that goal in secondary schools." The report goes on to state, "In reading and math, for instance, both the Latino-White gap and the gap between poor and nonpoor students grew or stayed the same in more states than they narrowed" (Education Trust, 2005, p. 2). A study undertaken by the Civil Rights Project at Harvard University (2006) predicts that by 2014, less than 50% of poor and minority students will achieve proficiency in mathematics on the NAEP tests if the current trend continues.

Closing the gap means overcoming many complex issues, such as expectations for students, underdeveloped language skills, teacher quality, and equity of resources and participation. Low expectations for poor and minority students continue to be a serious issue in our schools and communities. In their annual progress report on the alignment of high school policies with college and work, Achieve Inc. (2006) states: "Taking a challenging high school curriculum, including but not limited to Algebra II, cuts in half the gap in college completion rates between white students and African American and Latino students" (p. 13).

With this knowledge, instructional leaders must address the disparity in mathematics achievement by student subgroups in the context of a personalized, schoolwide improvement plan that specifically changes the culture around mathematics and numeracy in secondary schools.

Teenagers look to educators to "connect the dots" between course content and life.
Somewhere between the highly motivational discovery-based and interactive mathematics curriculum in the elementary school and the structured, rigorous secondary school mathematics preparation needed to pursue a technical or college career in science or mathematics, we lose the engagement and motivation of many of our students. Secondary students show little interest in and have no idea why (or what) mathematics courses are necessary for success in the university or workplace.

Addressing expectations of high school graduates in colleges and in the workplace must become a priority to fully assist middle level and high school students in preparing for their post–high school experiences. Schools must involve the postsecondary and business communities to ensure that the school standards are in alignment with their training and workplace expectations. As noted in *Closing the Expectations Gap 2006,*

"Postsecondary institutions must clearly define the skills that high school graduates need to be ready to take credit-bearing, nonremedial courses, and business leaders likewise must articulate the skills that graduates need to be successful and advance in their careers. High school standards then need to be anchored in these real-world expectations" (Achieve, 2006, p. 9).

To address this major disconnect between students' expectations and understanding of mathematics in the "real world," the following items should be considered:

- Employ inquiry-based problem-solving activities to link pedagogy and practice and to help students "connect the dots"
- Teach mathematics as a life skill and reinforce it in mathematics and content classes
- Teach problem-solving techniques and reinforce them in mathematics and content classes
- Gather community business support to reward students who continue their mathematics education throughout high school
- Value and teach mathematics competence, necessary to support a successful workforce, throughout the school
- Make students aware that accelerated mathematics classes lead to more satisfying employment and higher pay.

There is now, and will be in the foreseeable future, a shortage of qualified mathematics teachers getting students ready for the real world through mathematics preparation.

The shortage of qualified mathematics teachers has been an issue of deep concern for years. Since the early 1990s, the number of teachers leaving the profession has been greater than the number entering the profession (Sterling, 2004). The problem of identifying highly qualified mathematics teachers to fill these positions is three pronged. First, there is a genuine lack of trained individuals wishing to enter teaching, and of those entering teaching, fewer are mathematics majors. By some estimates, there will be a shortage of more than 280,000 mathematics and science teachers by 2015 (Business–Higher Education Forum, 2006) as individuals trained in these areas retire or seek more lucrative employment. Second, approximately 25% of teachers certified in other content areas are currently teaching mathematics and need to be either certified or replaced by qualified mathematics teachers. And, finally, as the shortage of mathematics teachers gets more and more crucial, districts are recruiting and hiring mathematics majors who lack teaching experience or educational coursework (Sterling, 2004).

The shortage of highly qualified mathematics teachers is especially critical in high-poverty/high-minority schools where students have a 50% chance of getting teachers in mathematics who hold neither a license nor a degree in the field and where the teacher turnover rate is twice as high as is in low-poverty schools (Sterling, 2004). In addition, in many schools, experienced mathematics teachers are assigned the advanced courses, leaving novice mathematics teachers instructing the students with the least preparation in and experience with mathematics.

- All students need a solid foundation in mathematics and should pursue higher-level mathematics courses.

- College and workplace expectations in support of increased mathematics rigor need to be clearly articulated.

- The shortage of qualified teachers will reduce the effectiveness of your school's mathematics program.
- Highly qualified teachers are needed across all courses, but particularly for high-poverty/high-minority students and those with low test scores.
- Special care must be taken to retain teachers just beginning their careers.
- For every student to be proficient in mathematics, every teacher must be fully involved.

Parents can be a tremendous source of support for the numeracy program. It is well known that parent involvement in schools and support for fledgling programs can make the difference between success and failure of an initiative. Further, as the National Parent Teachers Association will attest, when parents are involved, their children achieve more. It is important for you, as principal, to communicate early and often with families—inviting them to information-sharing sessions, sending newsletters with program updates and other important information, and participating in conferences and meetings to discuss the direct impact of higher expectations and increased mathematics rigor on their child. These meetings may provide a forum for parents and teachers to formulate and agree on a child's individual educational plan.

Principals need to stick together! A secondary school cannot expect to raise expectations, institute a rigorous curriculum, and increase student achievement around numeracy—or any other initiative—without the assistance of the education community. Well-crafted programs and ongoing parent education are essential to change the culture in support of the Numeracy Improvement Plan. Middle and high school principals should work together to present a united message to school faculties and the parental community by planning curricular changes and staff development activities that complement each other.

Stakeholders, such as central office personnel, college representatives, and business leaders—all who have vested interests in increased mathematics rigor—can be enlisted to support the numeracy efforts throughout the community through precollege programs and summer internships. Pull these individuals into the "inner circle" by offering information sessions where the goals and expected outcomes of the Numeracy Improvement Plan are discussed, and provide a variety of opportunities for them to become an integral part of the initiative.

Seven Action Items for Principals in Leading Schoolwide Numeracy Improvement

The principal is tasked with changing the school culture to embrace both a rigorous mathematics instruction program and the weaving of numeracy skills in every content area. This includes planning and participating in ongoing professional development sessions that renew and augment the curriculum standards and utilizing problem-solving techniques that reinforce and improve mathematics instruction across the curriculum.

To be viewed as a numeracy advocate and leader in the building, the principal must be seen by the teachers, parents, and students as committed to mathematics as a requisite and lifelong learning skill. You must be knowledgeable in hiring, training, and supporting, through professional development, highly qualified mathematics teachers who implement a quality standards-based mathematics curriculum. You must also hire and professionally support highly qualified subject-area teachers who integrate the mathematics of their content area into classroom applications that reflect real-life situations. You must be highly visible throughout the school, regularly visiting classrooms to ensure that numeracy truly is being implemented with real-world mathematics applications utilizing data and technology as tools. The following seven action items highlight these points and provide the structure for the upcoming chapters.

Action Item 1—Create a culture or change the existing culture to support numeracy.

■ *Increase the community's capacity for raising mathematics standards* by examining existing perceptions with the major community stakeholders and leading discussions about increased mathematics requirements for college and job-preparation demands.

■ *Increase the school's capacity for raising mathematics standards* by focusing the school staff on a vision of schoolwide numeracy to include yearlong concentrated efforts in all content areas, increased mathematics rigor for every student, and expansion of interdisciplinary opportunities in which students learn and practice mathematical skills.

Action Item 2—Establish collaborative teams that develop and implement a numeracy initiative to support and foster learning.

■ A numeracy team will play a critically important role by assisting the departmental teams in establishing common curriculum standards and implementing and aligning those standards to texts and tests. The numeracy team will identify resources, provide teacher support, and assume responsibility for writing the schoolwide Numeracy Improvement Plan. In addition, the numeracy team is responsible for data analysis of both schoolwide mathematics mastery and individual concept mastery that address mathematics achievement gaps.

■ School teams—department, grade level, and/or interdisciplinary—should be composed of highly motivated individuals who are capable of providing the leadership necessary for successful implementation of the Numeracy Improvement Plan. Since you are empowering collaborative teams, you should be sure that you provide adequate time for all teams to plan.

Action Item 3—Analyze mathematics assessment data to determine areas of instruction for schoolwide and individual student mathematics improvement.

■ *For schoolwide mathematics improvement* to occur, the numeracy team must collect and analyze multiple forms of school, teacher, and student data to identify the academic learning needs of students and the professional learning needs of teachers. A plan determining the mathematics strengths and weaknesses of the school, with input and collaboration from feeder schools, can allow the teachers to plan interdisciplinary activities and projects that will support and reinforce skills for the mathematics and content classes. Every teacher should be involved in analyzing, evaluating, and discussing student work.

■ *To determine the learning needs of individual students*, the numeracy team must examine the results of formative, summative, and teacher-prepared assessments to identify individual students who are scoring below grade level or below Proficient in mathematics, and analyze the data closely to identify specific skills the students must master to improve competency. These data, combined with less-formal information (e.g., grades, anecdotal records), should be used by the numeracy team to prepare a student's individual plan for mathematics progress.

Action Item 4—Initiate and monitor a rigorous mathematics curriculum for all students in every grade and implement rigorous mathematics instruction in every secondary classroom to support the skills, knowledge, and technology of the content area and to utilize problem-solving techniques.

■ *A standards-based rigorous mathematics curriculum must be made available to **every** student* in every secondary school. For students to compete successfully in today's job market, experience success in college, and be mathematically literate citizens, every opportunity should be given for secondary students to participate in all levels of mathematics. To achieve this goal, ongoing staff development with the entire faculty must occur to reinforce and refresh existing skills and introduce new concepts to be mastered.

■ *Mathematics instruction that supports content-area knowledge and skills, and uses technology and problem-solving techniques must be made available to **every** student* in every secondary school. To ensure that there will be rigor in all classrooms and that mathematics will be utilized as a problem-solving tool in every content area, the principal and the numeracy team must assess the training needs of staff, investigate opportunities for flexible scheduling to provide increased time for collaboration and instruction, and implement a student support plan.

■ *A crucial component for success is the highly visible monitoring of classrooms* to support and encourage implementation of rigorous mathematics content and comprehensive teaching strategies in every mathematics and content-area classroom.

Action Item 5—Hire highly qualified teachers who are familiar with the mathematics skills in their content area and foster ongoing professional development for all teachers to individualize and differentiate mathematics instruction for every student.

A successful mathematics program rests on the marriage of two factors: taking care to hire only the most highly qualified and talented teachers available in mathematics, as well as in other content areas, and presenting an effective, ongoing professional development program centered around building staff capacity to implement the goals of the Numeracy Improvement Plan. Together, the numeracy team and the principal must plan for job-embedded, peer-supported, research-based professional development throughout the year.

Action Item 6—Create a realistic budget for schoolwide numeracy.
The principal and school leaders, in collaboration with the numeracy team, should prioritize the needs of the school in implementing mathematics across all content areas. It is essential to determine what expenses need to be increased for schoolwide implementation to be effective. The principal must closely scrutinize the school budget allocation, additional district resources, contributions from community partnerships and outside agencies, and additional funding possibilities through grants that provide opportunities for mentors, summer programs, tutoring, and technology. Utilizing all of the resources available is essential to ensure full and ongoing support of the school's Numeracy Improvement Plan.

Action Item 7—Assess, through supervision, the effective use of personnel, time, and school and community resources.

The principal must demonstrate an unwavering commitment to the success of the schoolwide numeracy program through visibility and presence in the classrooms on a daily basis, coaching and encouraging both students and staff, while monitoring, evaluating, and giving honest feedback regarding the overall effectiveness of the schoolwide numeracy initiative. Your actions will bring full awareness to teachers as they address the achievement goals for their students.

Finally, at the end of each chapter is a checklist that will keep you and your team on track.

NOTES FROM THE FIELD …

Conrad Ball Middle School

Conrad Ball Middle School, located in Loveland, CO, is a school of nearly 800 students, 45% of whom are economically disadvantaged. Ball's principal, Diane Lauer, shares some of her thoughts on the significant increase in mathematics test scores at the school over the past five years.

Five years ago only one-third of our eighth grade students successfully completed a full year of Algebra I and two thirds completed half the course. Now, two-thirds of our students successfully complete a full year of Algebra I and one-third complete half the course. Our goal is to get all of our eighth graders into Algebra I, and that necessitates exceptional teaching and content knowledge.

A districtwide K–12 mathematics curriculum alignment and the decision to adopt a new mathematics text as well as do three years of job-embedded staff development were the initial steps that eventually led to significant changes in the instructional strategies used by teachers.

Strengthening our teachers' ability to differentiate in the math classroom has been an ongoing process. We are always tweaking and rethinking how to best serve students, whether in mixed groups or ability-based groups. Now our teachers are data savvy and can triangulate classroom assessments, grade-level assessments, and the results of the state assessment. Staff develop personal learning plans with their students through the use of data analysis, goal-setting techniques, and ongoing student self-assessment. Now our students are very savvy users of data and can independently set learning goals.

One of our major initiatives was to structure staff development and planning times. We identified vertical team meetings and content meetings as building priorities. The school structure provides teacher-planning and team-planning time each day. Teachers meet with their interdisciplinary groups three times per week and with their grade-level content teams one or two times a week. Math teachers collaborate in vertical teams once a month. This strengthens their ability to refine curriculum, analyze data, and evaluate instruction. Much work has been done in identifying the gaps between the texts we use and the state assessment frameworks. Teachers also use the time to create grade-level and departmental student achievement targets and the actions needed to meet the targets. Perhaps equally impressive, however, are the changes in the teachers themselves. Mathematics teachers meet weekly in professional learning communities to discuss common issues and support one another's teaching and learning. Teachers are

SCHOOL FACTS

**Conrad Ball
Middle School**

LOCATION:
Loveland, CO

SCHOOL DISTRICT:
Thompson R-2J

GRADE LEVELS:
6–8

POPULATION:
794

ECONOMICALLY
DISADVANTAGED:
41.3%

RACIAL/ETHNIC
GROUPS:
White 76.3%, Hispanic
20.6%, Black 1.0%,
American Indian 1.1%,
Asian 0.9%

able to sort classroom data to create flexible groups for differentiation and identify individual strengths and weaknesses, while monitoring the performance of one another's students to determine their own areas for personal growth.

Recent efforts have concentrated on developing a rigorous curriculum that embeds problem solving and integrated conceptual knowledge and utilizing a variety of instructional strategies to impact thinking skills, collaborative and inquiry learning, and oral/written articulation of mathematical thinking. As a school, we have implemented a "thinking strategies" initiative whereby teachers and students make connections; ask questions; determine importance; infer, visualize, and synthesize information across all content areas. We have found these strategies to be very valuable with regard to math instruction, especially since our state's math assessment necessitates strong problem-solving capabilities and the capacity to read, understand, and articulate mathematical thinking.

Finally, our other content-area teachers regularly support math instruction; this includes our exploratory, literacy, science, and social studies teachers. We strive to make connections to math, especially in the areas we know our students are most deficient.

The results speak for themselves: Conrad Ball has enjoyed a steady increase in mathematics achievement scores over the past five years and was designated the 2005 Colorado Trailblazer School to Watch by the National Forum to Accelerate Middle School Grades Reform and the Colorado Association of Middle Level Education.

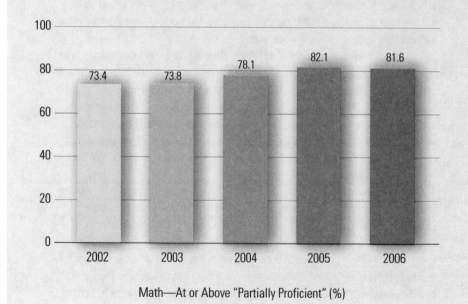

Math—At or Above "Partially Proficient" (%)

1 Creating a Numeracy Culture

If improving science and math education is suddenly a national priority, someone apparently forgot to tell the parents and students.

—Ben Feller, Education Reporter for the Associated Press

n many homes, schools, and communities, mathematics is viewed as an intellectual sieve, preparing top students for academic endeavors, and is not seen as a life skill whose application is required of all students in successful real-life situations. James Hunt, Jr., chairman of the Institute for Educational Leadership and Policy, agrees: "According to the latest poll conducted by Public Agenda, parents don't see the urgency of science and math" (Public Agenda, 2006). The poll, released in February 2006, finds 57% of parents believe that their child takes enough mathematics and science now (Johnson, Arumi, Oth, & Remaley, 2006) despite the predictions of the important role that mathematics will play in a competitive, technical global society. If students are to be successful in the future, all students must achieve a numeracy standard, and parents, teachers, and community members must support students who strive to master the mathematics concepts that are so critical to their success.

The current attitudes of acceptance regarding the characteristics of the limited number of students who are successful in mathematics and allowed to enroll in accelerated mathematics courses clearly indicate a need for a *culture change* for many parents and community members, as well as some staff members. Prior to implementation of a schoolwide numeracy program that encourages all students to enroll in more challenging mathematics courses and implements rigorous mathematics curriculum in all content areas, the school leader should create a common vision around the "culture of numeracy" in the school, one that is understood and supported by the community and by the parents and students. Because policymakers and employers can clearly see the importance of solid mathematics instruction in preparation for success in the work place, they may wish to work in partnership with school leaders and serve as the catalyst for changing the culture of numeracy with the stakeholders in the school community.

In environments where, often, many negative pressures exist to change other pressing educational outcomes at the school, increasing the number of students enrolled in mathematics courses and introducing rigor into the classroom is more likely to be ignored than to receive much resistance. Remarkably, more resistance is met in schools where many students are achieving. The Public Agenda survey indicates that large numbers of parents, as well as students, see no need for increased mathematics requirements. In the Public Agenda press release, Chairman Hunt goes on to point out, "There is a

Chapter 1:
Creating a Numeracy Culture

clear disconnect here. Policymakers and employers clearly see this slip as a threat to the nation's economy. But if our parents don't understand the importance, we can't expect our students to" (2006). It is interesting, as well as important, to recognize where the resistance comes from.

For example, Georgia O'Keeffe Middle School in Madison, WI, made the tough decision several years ago to do a "math makeover" by eliminating tracking for all students, establishing teaching teams, and introducing high-quality curriculum and instruction. Not surprisingly, most of the concerns were voiced mainly from middle-class parents who were unhappy that the school was dismantling the tracked system. As a result, the principal and staff, through a series of carefully crafted information dissemination activities, began a campaign to educate those parents and others who opposed the new approach to mathematics instruction. Although some vocal resistance by parents and other community members continued throughout the year, opposition faded away as test scores improved as a result of full implementation of the new program (Delmore, 2005).

The Public Agenda survey also revealed that "minority high schoolers are more likely to consider math and science 'absolutely essential' for 'real world success.'" In addition, "Black students are more likely to believe that kids are not being taught enough math and science and that it is a serious problem" (Johnson et al., 2006, p. 12). But does that mean that adolescents will be lining up to register for more mathematics classes and volunteering for the hard work of accelerated mathematics courses? Not likely. Students will only reluctantly begin to move toward difficult choices when they feel that the school culture, encouraged by parents and the community, will support them in this process.

Increasing the Community's Capacity for Raising Mathematics Standards

It is first the obligation of the principal and other school leaders to meet with community stakeholders early in the process to emphasize mathematics as an essential life skill for every student. To identify the position of the community stakeholders regarding this vision and to frame the vision discussion, all stakeholders should be asked to complete the Numeracy Capacity Survey (see Appendix 1) prior to the first meeting. The principal and the numeracy team should aggregate the survey results for presentation at that meeting. Demographic data of the school, such as the number of students enrolled in mathematics courses, the number of college freshmen needing remediation at the local or state university, and the mathematics skills needed for employment in the community and nationally, need to be collected for this meeting. Current research, such as that linking the number of accelerated mathematics classes completed with higher salaries, also should be prepared for dissemination. This information portrays mathematics preparation as the difference between just getting "a job" and gainful and productive employment. The survey results, research articles reinforcing the effectiveness of rigorous mathematics instruction, and demographic school statistics will most certainly ignite a lively discussion among the stakeholders about the importance of the mathematics preparation needed in middle and high school for success both in the current job market and in the preparation for university and postsecondary programs. (See Appendix 2 for resources.)

This discussion should culminate with the introduction of the concept of rigorous mathematics instruction in all content areas and the necessity for students to enroll in more accelerated mathematics classes. Finally, you should make the point that emphasis on a schoolwide culture of numeracy will be a major component of the school's systemic plan to create a supportive, encouraging, and challenging total learning environment for all students in both mathematics and reading.

Parents, with community business leaders, can become significant stakeholders in encouraging students to complete a rigorous K–12 mathematics curriculum, particularly when they see the correlation between the number of accelerated mathematics classes completed and getting and keeping a high-paying job. Share with them the results of an extensive longitudinal study completed in 2001 using the High School and Beyond survey data, where researchers Rose and Betts (2001) found that students who took higher level mathematics courses in high school were more likely to complete college and have higher incomes 10 years after high school graduation. Remarkably, this strong relationship held even after the researchers controlled for other student characteristics, such as ability.

The parents' role in increasing mathematics rigor through the schoolwide numeracy initiative should be encouraging, supportive, and active. One way the school can help facilitate engagement is through more productive use of the results of annual student assessments. Traditionally, assessment results are mailed to parents at the close of the school year. How each profile is used and interpreted by parents depends on the dedication to follow-up by the school as well as the parents' time, level of education, and other factors. This annual event presents an opportunity to help parents understand what mathematics content their child has mastered and has not mastered and what areas need to be addressed in the upcoming year. Through this activity, you can challenge parents to actively utilize this information to hold the school and classroom teachers accountable for addressing the mathematics content skills. This profile, usually underutilized by parents and the community, can become an individualized learning contract between parents and students and the school. As part of the overall culture change, individual assessment data can now be seen as a "to do" action plan rather than a "to file" document.

Parents, as well as teachers, will need to have access to best-practice instructional activities that will assist in closing the mathematics mastery gap at the school. The numeracy team and mathematics department may help in the identification of these materials with the support of state and local offices of instruction, recommendations from subject-area organizations and review of Web-based resources. Many benchmark assessment resources give sample mathematics questions and a selection of Web links to effective mathematics activities that can be used by the parents, teachers, or the student seeking mastery. Linking areas of nonmathematics mastery with proven instructional activities is an excellent resource for faculty members, students, and parents who want improved mathematics skills as tested by the state assessments.

The state of Ohio, in many ways, has taken a lead in providing schools with resources aligned to all of the content areas. Through the Data Driven Decisions Academic Achievement initiative (www.d3a2.org), users from the Ohio educational community will be able to access tools to help analyze school, classroom, and individual student data. To address needs identified through a thorough data analysis, educators can retrieve online resources provided by the system, such as lesson plans and assessments aligned to Ohio's Academic Content Standards.

An additional culture change occurs when teachers in all content areas are encouraged to utilize classroom activities that emphasize problem-solving techniques in real-life situations. This shift may require discussion with parents to help them understand the need for students to have skills in estimation, logical arguments and fallacies, data interpretation, team participation, and effective use of technology. It may also provide an opportunity to help prepare parents who are trying to support students with these activities. The Numeracy Capacity Survey provides an opportunity for all stakeholders to discuss the long-term vision of numeracy for all students, what it looks like at the university or workforce level, what quality classroom activities include, and what advantages numeracy adds to the future success of their students.

As students adapt to the increased mathematics rigor in every classroom or are given opportunities to participate in additional mathematics electives, an informed school community must continue to encourage, support, and be involved in the enhanced teacher efforts and the increased student efforts.

Increasing the School's Capacity for Raising Mathematics Standards

Prior to initiating a schoolwide numeracy program, all faculty members should also complete the Numeracy Capacity Survey, examine the aggregated results, and discuss the schoolwide impact. It is central to the success of the initiative for the faculty to formulate a strong vision of the necessity for all students to meet rigorous mathematics standards to be competitive in university or postsecondary programs and in the workforce. As in the preparation for your community meetings, demographic data, research articles, and the survey results should be gathered for this meeting as well as a summary of the commitment and results of the community meeting. This information will help the staff focus on the vision of schoolwide numeracy, concentrate efforts on content activities that teach collaborative problem solving, and reinforce interdisciplinary opportunities to utilize mathematics tools. The faculty discussion must center on ways to increase mathematics rigor for every student, each year, at the middle and high school levels. It will begin the conversation among stakeholders around "What we want as a successful school versus what we currently have." The data can provide information to identify areas of numeracy strength for the school and areas in need of improvement. It can be utilized as the catalyst to spark conversations among staff about the need for increasing academic rigor in all classrooms, addressing real-life problems, and providing activities that utilize mathematics tools for problem solving in all content areas. Armed with information, research, survey results, and the shared vision developed with community stakeholders, the school leadership team with the support of the numeracy team will be ready to launch the process that will ultimately lead to schoolwide improvement in mathematics instructional practices and increased student achievement.

Quality instruction in each subject area involves identifying and utilizing the mathematics content embedded in their fields and utilizing the technology tools that support these activities. Moving a faculty toward project-based learning informed by assessment data is a powerful but challenging change in culture. The instructional leadership team will need to identify professional development activities that support the staff in planning or selecting authentic instructional activities such as utilizing mathematics as a problem-solving tool, facilitating student work groups, and supporting and reinforcing student efforts toward mathematics skill mastery.

Staff must also be actively involved in fulfilling the "contract" with parents springing from the individual assessment profile mailed to parents in the spring or summer. Parents may begin asking for embedded instruction in the content area to further develop mathematics skills and for support in areas where students have not mastered concepts and skills related to mathematics in the content areas. Consequently, all teachers must be able to identify activities and resources that will help students learn mathematics skills in their subject areas. These activities can be identified by the numeracy team, by the district, and/or through teacher discussions and planning.

Determining What Academic Rigor Looks Like

A good way to begin preparation for the new school year is to ask your staff this question: "What is academic rigor?" Before beginning the discussion, read the following quote:

Chapter 1:
Creating a Numeracy Culture

> *This dichotomy of thought, that we should improve high school education but not change the basic structure of the educational process, is even more perplexing when you realize that high schools are hard pressed to define what the intended result— the educated student—looks like. Most high school officials are not able to describe in holistic terms what a graduate knows and is able to do, but they can tell you what the students "took," how many credits the student earned, and what student did it best. (Gainey and Webb, 1998, p. 1)*

Then, ask your staff to come to consensus in defining academic rigor. Appendix 3 contains suggestions for directing this process so that each individual has an opportunity for input. Unless the faculty is small, it may not be logistically possible to form one working group and create one final definition. You can display the three or four definitions (from groups of 20 or more) on chart paper and open discussion to all staff members about similarities and differences. It is possible to reach one consensus definition from this discussion. Discuss each of the phrases in the definition(s) and what each means to the faculty. Under the leadership of Principal Greg Spradling, the 100 faculty members at Durango (CO) High School participated in this exercise during a professional development opportunity at their school. The faculty discussion, centered around four definitions of academic rigor, generated the following list:

- Academic rigor is work that challenges and engages individual students to climb their ladders of individual potential.
- Consistently challenge students to learn, understand, synthesize, and apply meaningful, in-depth, and complex content.
- Academic rigor is differentiated, accessible levels of learning that engage and stimulate each student to apply constant thinking skills to real-world problems and to rise to his or her full potential.
- When each student is challenged to produce measurable results that require self-discipline and creativity to successfully negotiate complex situations.
- Presenting material that is challenging in all developmental areas of student growth (physical, emotional, spiritual)—guiding the student through the material with assistance and supplemental support to access their highest potential as a lifelong learner.

- Students and their learning communities hold themselves accountable through apt assessments for maximizing their individualized learning and continually reaching higher expectations.

- Providing a juggernaut of knowledge and experience in a subject area that is challenging to each student individually without relying on arbitrary markers; not a one-size-fits-all model.

- Challenging, meaningful, yet attainable content that encourages the students to utilize multiple cognitive skills to go beyond what they think they can achieve

- Teachers provide an instructional roadmap for students that creates meaningful, relevant instruction that challenges students beyond standards to the mastery level of learning so that they think "outside of the box" and are able to synthesize multiple levels of information. This will result in an increased and more sophisticated knowledge base to enrich and improve lifelong learning.

The consensus definition was formulated from a discussion of the common words or phrases in each definition:

- Challenging
- Meaningful
- Individual
- Lifelong learner
- Skills/standards/multiple learning
- Students.

The next step is to ask your staff: "As an evaluator, when I come into your academically rigorous classroom, what teacher behaviors will I see? What student behaviors will I see?" This brainstorming activity at Durango generated the following lists:

Identified Teacher Behaviors	Identified Student Behaviors
Encouraging	Questioning
Modeling	Discussing
Engaged	Creating
Coaching	Discovering
Questioning	Thinking
Moving	Exploring
Listening	Changing
Using opportunities	Demonstrating
Laughing	Listening
Connecting	
Challenging	
Interacting	

The next challenge was for the Durango departmental teams to lead the discussion around what specific teacher behaviors and student behaviors an evaluator would observe in an academically rigorous mathematics classroom, social studies classroom, physical education classroom, and so forth. This activity is particularly powerful when used with a highly motivated and engaged staff. The administrative team may also have subdivided the faculty by grade levels rather than departments and led the discussion around the specific teacher behaviors and student behaviors that an evaluator would observe in an academically rigorous seventh-grade classroom. Taking this next step, the Durango faculty generated a list of teacher and student behaviors for their departments. A sample follows:

ENGLISH

English department academic rigor definition: Academic rigor in the English department is expecting more of students than they expect of themselves.

Teacher behaviors:

- Modeling reading, writing, vocabulary, and thinking strategies
- Monitoring student use of thinking, reading, and writing strategies
- Coaching and differentiating for students their use of thinking, reading, and writing strategies
- Conferring with students about their reading, writing, and thinking strategies
- Encouraging students to try new writing and reading strategies
- Moving through the room to individualize work for students and to engage them in activities
- Facilitating group discussions
- Listening to students' thinking about reading and writing and then responding to them
- Questioning students' thinking
- Connecting with students about issues in texts, in their writing, and in the world
- Sharing their experiences as readers and writers
- Interacting with students about their thinking on reading and writing, even laughing together with them.

Student behaviors:

- Writing, revising, and rewriting
- Self-evaluating reading, writing, thinking, and listening skills (being metacognitive)
- Thinking critically about reading and writing:
  - ❏ Inquiring/asking questions
  - ❏ Interpreting/inferring
  - ❏ Creating and synthesizing
- Reading to understand/for understanding
- Producing an individually appropriate product of reading and writing
- Engaging actively in discussion and activities for reading, writing, and thinking
- Trying new strategies of reading and writing and revising
- Expressing themselves creating through speaking and writing

SCHOOL FACTS

Durango High School

LOCATION:
Durango, CO

SCHOOL DISTRICT:
Durango 9-R

GRADE LEVELS:
9–12

POPULATION:
1,479

ECONOMICALLY DISADVANTAGED:
15.2%

RACIAL/ETHNIC GROUPS:
White 82.7%, Hispanic 11.2%, Native American 4.3%, Black 0.6%, Asian 1.0%

The "what does rigor look like" lists will spark conversation around what motivated learning looks like and will help focus the exchange of ideas on student competencies and teacher behaviors. Discussion ideas associated with higher-order thinking, problem-solving techniques, questioning, teaming, student engagement, personalized learning, equity of participation, and diversified learning—and what, in particular, these behaviors look like in each content-area classroom—can easily become a part of the conversation. These observable behaviors serve as the basis for models of rigor that can:

- Provide teachers with concrete examples of rigorous instruction
- Motivate student learning
- Increase the depth of student understanding
- Accommodate different learning styles
- Teach the application of mathematics and problem solving in the content areas
- Integrate technology tools into the classroom.

The principal should secure a commitment from all classroom teachers to do their best to raise expectations, implement high curriculum standards, and continue to utilize instructional models that produce the desired student and teacher behaviors in their classrooms every day. The administrative team is responsible for monitoring both instruction and instructional delivery through classroom observation and teacher evaluation. Implementing a lesson that meets the curriculum standards of the grade-level or departmental course does not necessarily meet the criteria necessary to diversify learning, encourage problem-solving techniques, simulate real-life situations, and motivate students to be engaged. The behaviors identified in the "what does rigor look like" lists will go a long way to move the conversation to instructional delivery for individual student success, and these behaviors are the ones that the principal, administrators, and leadership team members need to be looking for in each visit to a "rigorous classroom."

Creating a School Culture for Teaching and Learning

While you are reshaping the culture of your school around who is responsible for teaching mathematics concepts and who is taking accelerated mathematics classes and why, include opportunities for rich conversations about student work and student progress. In fact, the next activity that your teams and departments should explore is, What does academic mathematics rigor look like in the content classroom? In departmental teams, ask the staff to review their curriculum standards and identify standards that support or utilize embedded mathematics skills. Next, review the departmental or grade-level definitions of academic rigor and then generate additions to their teacher behavior and student behavior lists that would be observed in the content classroom that supports embedded mathematics activities. Additions to the list may include problem solving, looking at graphs, integrating technology, etc. Directions for monitoring this process would be similar to those described previously in this chapter and in Appendix 3.

In order to achieve the desired behaviors, you need to move from "prose" to "practice." Provide opportunities for teachers to observe best practices and participate in interdisciplinary team-teaching activities. Teachers must have time to discuss, plan, practice, share, and reason through the issues surrounding mathematics, rigorous instruction, and student progress. Reshape the school environment so that parents, students, and teachers can collaborate and share decisions about student learning.

Give teachers a formal opportunity to evaluate and discuss the specific details of the numeracy initiative and how it has affected them and the progress of their students. Plan regular roundtable discussions for teachers about what is working well and what may need readjustment. Discuss ways to improve teaching strategies and celebrate and acknowledge ways that the program and teachers have been effective.

Student learning and teacher planning for learning take time. Be flexible and creative. Put your faculty meeting in a bulletin and plan a meeting around instruction and student outcomes. Provide flexible scheduling during the school day that gives extended time for increased mathematics instruction, collaborative teacher planning, student practice and engagement, and evaluation of instruction. Remember, the schedule does not drive the school; teaching and learning drive the schedule.

NOTES FROM THE FIELD...

Campbell Middle School

Campbell Middle School, which is 64% minority students and 34% economically disadvantaged students, is located in the Cypress-Fairbanks Independent School District in Houston, TX. Faced with declining mathematics test scores (2002, 2003, 2004), Campbell employed a multifaceted approach to addressing improvement in mathematics for its 1,400 students. Adopting the philosophy that all of their students can achieve at a higher level, Principal Robert Hatcher and the Campbell teachers implemented the initiatives described below, directly addressing rigor in the classroom:

- Discovery lessons were designed by teachers to ensure that students were truly mastering the concepts presented, and less time was spent on rote drill assignments

- Mathematics support programs, including emphasis on mathematics vocabulary in all classrooms, were instituted by teachers

- Vertical planning was instituted so teachers could build a more coherent mathematics curriculum by grade level and in subsequent grades

- Questioning strategies were employed by teachers to ensure that they were extending student learning through more open-ended, higher-level questions

- Technology, such as SmartBoards, computer software, and graphing calculators, was utilized more often for the presentation of material and reinforcement of learning

- Real-life connections were made through the enrichment of students' mathematics vocabulary and narration of stories that related to real-world situations and applications

- Goal-setting conferences were held by teachers who met with students to review the previous year's performance on assessments and to set goals for the current year.

In addition to the classroom implementation, schoolwide support for these initiatives is apparent. Through the Advisory Outreach Program, students who failed the mathematics portion of the state assessment were given additional support in mathematics during the daily advisory class period; students who scored below the minimum passing rate were identified for a mentoring program to address individual needs in and out of the classroom; teachers, with assistance from high school students, organized and tutored students in groups established using data from the tested objectives. As a result of these efforts, Campbell students showed significant progress on the Texas Assessment of Knowledge and Skills, overall and in all subgroups.

Subgroup	% Passing rate		Difference
	2005	2006	
All	62	71	9
Asian American	40	55	15
Hispanic	53	64	11
White	74	79	5
Economically disadvantaged	50	59	9

THE PRINCIPAL'S CHECKLIST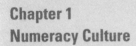

Chapter 1
Numeracy Culture

Parent and Community Support

_____ Identify community stakeholders, including parents, business, and university partners

_____ Identify alliances

_____ Alert community stakeholders to numeracy initiative vision

_____ Administer and collect the Numeracy Capacity Survey

_____ Aggregate and analyze survey results

_____ Gather:

    _____ Survey results

    _____ Demographic data

    _____ Current research, including job trends

    _____ Local college and university placement data

_____ Introduce a vision for more rigorous mathematics instruction, more students enrolled in accelerated mathematics

_____ Schedule and hold first information-sharing meeting.

_____ Facilitate the discussion at parent meetings around the formulation of a strong numeracy vision and the behaviors that move the vision into practice for the school

_____ Distribute student assessment profiles to parents

_____ Prepare and distribute best-practices materials for parents to assist their students in areas of weakness

_____ Hold student-parent conferences to design a contract between home and school

_____ Hold meetings to assist parents with mathematics concepts and skills.

Faculty Support

_____ Administer and collect the Numeracy Capacity Survey

_____ Aggregate and analyze survey results

_____ Discuss schoolwide improvement with leadership and numeracy teams

_____ Discuss schoolwide improvement with full faculty and staff

_____ Present demographic data, research, survey results, and community stakeholders' vision at a faculty meeting

_____ Facilitate (or delegate) the discussion around the formulation of a strong numeracy vision for the school

_____ Develop a consensus schoolwide numeracy vision.

2 Collaborative Leadership in Support of Numeracy

True collaboration is a discipline—a fragile, high-maintenance set of practices and attitudes that needs constant care and attention.

—Mike Schmoker

The principal plays a dynamic role in shaping the teaching and learning environments in the school. By understanding and appreciating the importance of mathematics to the life of the community and its children; by organizing and sharing resources of all sorts with teachers, parents, and students; and by actively encouraging each teacher's use of a variety of learning strategies, the principal becomes an indispensable partner in transforming the current learning environment into a culture of numeracy.

Principals cannot "go it alone." There are many compelling reasons for principals to cultivate good working relationships with the teachers in their buildings. Relying exclusively on the principal as the sole leader—regardless of the commitment to or capacity for reform—will lead to the creation of a few high-performing schools within systems that not only allow, but often perpetuate, mediocrity. Leadership comes from numerous places beyond the principal's office: teachers, parents, students, support staff, community/business representatives, and other stakeholders.

The principal will find that the best work is done with teachers in collaborative teams that support and foster learning and provide significant opportunities for decision making, all of which will lead to improvements in instructional practice and support school improvement. High-quality collaboration efforts provide the groundwork for easy access to information by all parties and present opportunities for teachers in different disciplines to communicate with each other, recognizing the importance of subject areas beyond their own.

The Value of a High-Performance Team

For the most sweeping, schoolwide impact, you must be willing to organize the school into *high-performance teams*. Ideally, when appointed, a *real team* is a group of individuals with complementary skills, and the team members are equally committed to common purposes, goals, and a working approach for which they hold themselves accountable. Your aim is to transform a real team into a high-performance team, which has all the characteristics of a real team plus the members' deep commitment to one another's personal growth and success. Because this type of team significantly outperforms all other teams, the high-performance team serves as a model as you structure your school teams.

All of your high-performance team members should have high energy and perseverance as well as the ability to shake up the status quo and "make things happen" for the secondary student. Since teams will serve as a catalyst for school change, only highly motivated, respected, and dedicated teachers should be selected for the pivotal leadership teams—teachers committed to their own growth as well as to the growth of the school. Principal style, school custom/tradition, and strength of school staff will determine the best method to choose team members to make up the various groups.

Characteristics of High-Performance Teams

Regardless of how team members are selected—volunteered, elected, invited, appointed—high-performance team members should possess most of the following traits:

- A commitment to growth and development

- A reputation for innovation

- An ability to make things happen

- Evidence of energy and persistence

- Demonstrated leadership ability

- A willingness to work

- Patience

- Respect of the faculty

- Small- and large-group communication skills.

Painter, Lucas, Wooderson, and Valentine (2000, p. 4)

Building and Empowering the High-Performance Numeracy Team

The first action in implementing a successful school initiative is the principal's selection and appointment of members of a high-performance numeracy team. This team comprises highly motivated, respected, and committed administrators, content teachers, resource teachers, data specialists, and representative stakeholders (i.e., parent, student, and/or business representatives) who value collaboration. This team is supported by exemplary mathematics resource teachers and perhaps a counselor or other individual who identifies and schedules students into content classes. Team members should be highly skilled and totally committed to increasing numeracy for *every* student. The team plays a fundamental role in identifying a schoolwide numeracy improvement vision, implementing a rigorous curriculum, locating resources and instructional activities for implementation, and providing teacher support for differentiating instruction and utilizing problem-based, real-life activities. The numeracy team looks at schoolwide assessments, plans mathematics improvement strategies, and writes the school Numeracy Improvement Plan. It is concerned with improving mathematics mastery and instruction in all content areas and with identifying professional development activities that will renew the professional skills of highly qualified and high-performing teachers.

Since the numeracy initiative will impact all instructional areas of the school, the numeracy team must be composed of representatives from existing school structures:

- *Administrative or leadership teams,* composed of individuals who influence the direction of the school's instructional program and plan and monitor the implementation of the instructional activities in each content area by frequent classroom visitation. The numeracy team should have a liaison from this group.

- *Departments* in each content area, supported by highly motivated members of the mathematics staff, may be instrumental in identifying and understanding the requisite mathematics skills embedded in each of the content areas. Departmental members must be committed to assisting in the development of instructional activities and projects that embed mathematics skills in the content of each subject area. The numeracy team should have a representative from each content area.

- *Grade levels,* consisting of highly motivated content-area teachers, provide an interdisciplinary opportunity for teachers. Through this structure, teachers may reinforce mathematics skills across the entire instructional program and fully integrate numeracy strategies. If this structure exists in your school, representatives should be included on the numeracy team.

The purpose of the numeracy team is to influence the direction of the school's instructional program by analyzing data to identify schoolwide weaknesses in mathematics skills and by recommending the instructional activities in each content area that will strengthen these skills. This team will disaggregate school data by analyzing three- to five-year trends, mastery or nonmastery of mathematics skills group data, and the recent annual assessment data for the school. They are also responsible for analyzing assessment data for individual students during the year, including review of individual student assessment profiles and results from teacher-made assessments. (See Chapter 3). The team will meet with the grade-level instructional teams and/or department members to prepare activities for large- and small-group instruction for students, with a focus on reinforcing the learning of specific mathematics skills. In addition, they are charged with identifying the professional learning needs of the staff for successful implementation of the Numeracy Improvement Plan.

From the beginning, the success of the numeracy team will be based on your support and the support of the teaching staff. The numeracy team must look and feel empowered to make significant changes in the instructional program to enhance student learning through the integration of mathematics skills in every content area.

Strategies for principals that empower and encourage commitment include:

- Finding time for numeracy team collaborative planning
- Reorganizing the master schedule to create common departmental or grade-level planning times
- Providing opportunities for department and grade-level teachers to give input into the numeracy plan and its implementation
- Protecting teacher instructional time by limiting announcements and classroom interruptions
- Encouraging and facilitating peer observation
- Celebrating achievements, recognizing successful projects and activities and making them available to other teachers
- Monitoring numeracy plan implementation and discussing during faculty and parent meetings
- Promoting high-quality work, student engagement, technology integration, and activities with real-life applications of mathematics skills
- Requiring all teachers to accommodate different learning styles and individualizing activities to improve each student's mathematics skill mastery
- Reducing implementation stress by emphasizing depth over breadth in curriculum, defining specific planning and meeting times, distributing best-practice activities, and providing targeted professional development
- Using parent volunteers, substitutes, and creative scheduling to release teachers for strategic planning.

Creating the Numeracy Improvement Plan

Once convened, the numeracy team accepts the responsibility to develop a Numeracy Improvement Plan—an important component of the School Improvement Plan—that concentrates on strategies to improve numeracy skills in all content areas. You must empower each team member to carefully analyze school standardized test results and mathematics assessment data, detect achievement gaps in mathematics mastery, identify content curriculum that can reinforce skills mastery, identify need-based professional development, provide resources for interdisciplinary activities and projects, and recommend yearlong small- and large-group student support activities.

Laying a foundation to plan

A basic tenet of this initiative is that numeracy is an ongoing priority for the entire school, at all levels and in all grades. Until recently, numeracy has been seen as just a short list of some basic mathematical skills that all students need to master by the close of their high school years. We are just beginning to realize that in our complex lives, outside of the formal educational setting—at home, at work, and in the community—we need to have a wider variety of mathematical skills and reasoning concepts and techniques in our personal toolkits. Although it is still tremendously important to maintain rigorous and challenging mathematics classes at every level, numeracy concepts must also be taught and reinforced in all classrooms.

The administrative and numeracy teams in schools wishing to institute a schoolwide numeracy program should first familiarize themselves with the latest developments in mathematics and numeracy education. Preliminary discussions and focused study groups can do much to bring staff members up-to-speed on current issues and dispel much of the anxiety that accompanies any major change in school culture. After reflecting on school data and practice and making a judgment about current school performance, the numeracy team must act as the catalyst for improved mathematics instruction in the school.

As your school team writes the School Improvement Plan section on numeracy, it will need to identify the following resources critical to the gathering of important data for this document:

- Schoolwide mathematics mastery objectives by grade level
- Instructional materials in all content areas that reinforce mathematics skills
- Staff development needs of teachers to support differentiated instruction
- Individual student data for small- and large-group instruction
- Real-life problem-solving activities that are interdisciplinary in nature and include projects that utilize mathematics and technology as tools
- Available technology that can be utilized both as an instructional and/or a management tool
- Opportunities for yearlong mathematics learning and support opportunities for teachers and students.

Use these resources to establish a context for conversations about school needs, to develop a sense of *vision* for the overall initiative, and to establish the overarching *goals*. As you would do with individual student data, develop clear statements about where the school is, where it would like to be, and what short-term (current year) and long-term actions might get it there. Expand this view to include noninstructional areas such as related school policies, school operations, and/or the evaluation system. Create opportunities for staff members to discuss standards for quality student work.

These actions, which may have been worked out in advance within the numeracy team, must be prioritized with whole-staff engagement through large- or small-group discussions or other processes to be successful. Although this phase may seem relatively simple, it must be well designed to ensure that the ultimate product—the Numeracy Improvement Plan—is thorough, comprehensive, and manageable.

This preplanning encompasses the first two of the four broad steps in the Numeracy Improvement Plan cycle:

1. **Analyzing the current situation** involves researching numeracy best practices, identifying current priorities in the school, and conceptualizing new "improved" practices
2. **Deciding what needs to be done** includes locating information, choosing the data to be gathered, and establishing needs and actions (see "Data Collected to Complete the School Numeracy Profile" in Chapter 3)
3. **Developing the Numeracy Improvement Plan**
4. **Establishing a continual cycle of review**.

A straightforward method of approaching the actual development of the Numeracy Improvement Plan involves separating the task into the two manageable components described here.

Numeracy teaching and learning

The result of conversations between the leadership and numeracy teams, and among the staff as a whole, around *school beliefs and vision* serves as an introduction to the plan. This section may include shared understandings about teaching and learning, the school community's view of numeracy, or an articulation of the value of numeracy as fundamental to the achievement of educational outcomes for the students.

Also included in this narrative are the broad *numeracy goals* for the total school population. Examples of numeracy goals are:

■ To enable all students to master the standards set forth in the Mathematics Framework

■ To provide numerous opportunities for all students to understand how mathematics is connected to the world outside of school.

Finally, this first section is the place to summarize the *current status* of the numeracy instructional program at the school. A listing of current priorities, instructional strategies, and existing programs and projects, as well as all related activities that may include parents and the business community, should be described in detail. This section might also include a description of the mathematics/numeracy curriculum, an overview of the school's general teaching and learning in this area, current sources of assessment information and professional development activities.

Student numeracy achievement

In this section, the numeracy team focuses specifically on school and student strengths and weaknesses on state or local assessments, as identified through a thorough analysis of general school population mathematics test results and results gleaned from a detailed study of both *mathematics* course and class-specific *student performance data*. School data collected should include mathematics courses completed, final grades, benchmark exams, and so forth. Several types of subgroup analyses should be performed on both sets of data: by year, by gender, by race, by economic status, and by program (English-language learners, gifted and talented, special education, and other school groups). Cohort progress over time and year-to-year comparisons should be examined.

Another source of data is that collected from a detailed review of *numeracy applications in nonmathematics content areas*. Depending on the current status of numeracy efforts across the curriculum, this review might identify strengths and weaknesses in such areas as the willingness and confidence with which students use mathematics outside the mathematics classroom or the capacity of the teachers to employ numeracy activities in their content areas. Data in this area can be gathered in several different ways: student and staff interviews or surveys, curriculum review, assessment data analyses in nonmathematics content areas, business community feedback, and college/university remedial-class data review. A suggested template to organize these data can be found in Appendix 4.

The numeracy team should look at these four sets of results (general school assessment data, specific student subgroup assessment data, general mathematics subject area/class performance data, and mathematics data from other content areas) to compile the *School Numeracy Profile* which identifies common mathematics patterns; areas of strength; areas of weakness; and other, perhaps unexpected, outcomes that may surface.

The last step in formulating a living Numeracy Improvement Plan involves planning and creating individual students' *Personal Plan for Mathematics Proficiency* (PP4MP). The numeracy team is charged with reviewing individual student data, identifying students in need of assistance, and mapping out an individualized plan of action. Ideally, each of the identified student's teachers should be involved in the development of this plan with the student and parent. A member of the school staff (i.e., mathematics teacher, counselor, team member) is charged with ongoing supervision of assigned students and for conducting periodic review sessions with the student's teachers for monitoring purposes and plan modifications, as needed.

This extensive schoolwide and individual data gathering and analysis must spawn *action plans in the areas of priority*. The format of these plans should be determined by the numeracy team, with practical input by members of the mathematics and other content-area departments, and approved by the principal and leadership team.

Suggested components of the action template include:

Chapter 2: Collaborative Leadership in Support of Numeracy

- Priority area information—rationale for action, short- and long-term target goals, and monitoring criteria
- Action to be taken—what is to be done, by whom, and within what time frame
- Resources needed—human, material, and/or teacher development
- Funding considerations—costs, sources of funds, grant opportunities, in-kind contributions.

See Appendix 5 for a sample template.

Monitoring, reviewing, and evaluating the plan

As with the overall school plan, the portion of the plan containing numeracy goals and objectives may be constantly revised during the school year on the basis of periodic benchmark testing results measured against growth and mastery in mathematics. The monitoring effort must be enthusiastically led by members of both the numeracy team (employing support through peer observation) and the administrative team (conducting classroom and teacher observations and evaluations). All individuals must be committed to the implementation of an effective numeracy program and driven by the desire for increased student achievement. The Numeracy Improvement Plan must establish a realistic timeline and build in the periodic monitoring activities. The final evaluation of the initiative should occur, at minimum, on an annual basis. The team must take care to devise appropriate evaluation criteria and strategies at the beginning of the cycle so that all stakeholders will understand what will be evaluated, how it will be evaluated, and when the evaluation will take place. The Numeracy Improvement Plan results will be made public as part of the overall School Improvement Plan.

The purpose of the Numeracy Improvement Plan evaluation is to provide information that will be useful in gauging the school's improvement in the area of mathematics and numeracy and identifying areas for improvement. A useful report will:

- Describe the methods of evaluation
- Utilize a variety of data—quantitative (achievement), perceptual (interviews, surveys, focus groups), and trend (comparing year-by-year results, school and classroom data)

- Employ visual aids (charts, tables, graphs) to display data
- Compare goals and objectives with accomplishments
- Communicate findings effectively
- Identify areas where action may be taken.

Finally, the School Improvement Plan, with its literacy and numeracy initiative components, should not be stored in a binder in the "vinyl museum" in the principal's office. This plan should be distributed to every stakeholder and treated as a living document that is monitored and evaluated throughout the school year. The plan should encompass formative evaluations with a final summative evaluation at the end of the year, informed by current classroom and assessment data.

Numeracy Team

_____ Identify, select, and appoint members of the numeracy team

_____ Find time for numeracy team collaborative planning

_____ Assist the team in becoming familiar with the latest developments in mathematics and numeracy education

_____ Identify resources critical to gathering data for the numeracy section of the School Improvement Plan

_____ Develop the numeracy vision and goals with the numeracy team.

Staff

_____ Revise and prioritize the vision and goals through total staff engagement

_____ Provide opportunities for teachers to give input into the numeracy plan

_____ Provide opportunities for teachers to discuss the numeracy plan implementation on an ongoing basis.

Numeracy Plan

_____ Assist the numeracy team with developing a process to formulate the numeracy plan, including:

    _____ Analyzing the current situation

    _____ Deciding what needs to be done—analyzing the school numeracy profile (see Chapter 3)

    _____ Developing the plan

    _____ Establishing a continual cycle of review

    _____ Planning and creating Personal Plan for Mathematics Proficiency for students

_____ Develop a process to monitor the numeracy plan implementation

_____ Devise a process to distribute the School Improvement Plan, including numeracy and literacy components, to all stakeholders.

Demonstrated Commitment

_____ Review the master schedule for ways to create common planning time

_____ Protect instructional time by limiting announcements and other interruptions

_____ Encourage and facilitate peer observation

_____ Celebrate achievements, recognize successful projects, and make them available to other teachers

_____ Define collaboratively with staff:

    _____ High-quality work

    _____ Student engagement

    _____ Technology integration

    _____ Activities with real-life applications of mathematics skills.

_____ Reduce implementation stress by:
     _____ Emphasizing depth over breath in curriculum
     _____ Defining specific planning and meeting times
     _____ Distributing best-practices activities
     _____ Providing targeted professional development
_____ Use parent volunteers, substitutes, and creative scheduling to release teachers for strategic planning.

3 Analyzing Data for Schoolwide and Individual Student Improvement

What separates the schools that will be successful in their reform efforts from the ones that won't is the use of one, often neglected, essential element—data.

—*Victoria Bernhardt*

The principal must make effective use of student performance data to identify and guide all instructional decisions—most especially for those decisions influencing school improvement. "When teachers and administrators examine data as part of the school improvement process, school improvement teams become more efficient and effective, decision making becomes more collaborative, teachers develop more positive attitudes about their own and their students' abilities, and educators begin to feel more in charge of their own destinies," according to Craig Jerald in a 2006 brief on collecting and using data to increase student achievement (p. 2). Assessment data empower teachers to make informed instructional choices. The analysis of external and internal assessments by the numeracy team not only can support differentiated instruction but also can identify potential interdisciplinary mathematics instructional topics and professional development needs and set schoolwide goals to leverage improvement in mathematics. The team should analyze *three to five years of data* to establish the mastery and nonmastery trends.

Analyzing Data to Complete the School Numeracy Profile

The outcome of the numeracy team data study will be to capture the *School Numeracy Profile*, a powerful tool in defining schoolwide numeracy initiatives and in committing the resources necessary to guide improvement. The School Numeracy Profile is a summary of the mathematics content standards mastered or not mastered by each grade level and by each of the 10 subgroups required for federal reporting. However, the depth of data analysis should go beyond just reviewing standardized data. Members of the numeracy team are tasked with collecting and analyzing multiple forms of student, school, and teacher data to identify the mathematics learning needs of student groups and then to identify the professional learning needs of the teachers. The School Numeracy Profile analyzes and interprets trends in four types of schoolwide data: perceptual, summative, formative, and demographic. Principals who have no experience analyzing this type of school data might consider seeking professional development in this area through district or state resources.

Perceptual data

Perceptual data reflect the opinions and views of stakeholders concerning the school culture, much like the Numeracy Capacity Survey (Appendix 1) completed by all stakeholders. Before the staff discusses the findings in the School Numeracy Profile, all staff members should be given an opportunity, in focus groups, meetings, or conferences, to discuss their perceptions about why individual student groups have achieved Proficient or above in mathematics on assessment tests and why other student groups have not. As a staff, investigate and record the answers to key questions such as:

- What do I think it would take for every subgroup (economically disadvantaged, Hispanic, etc.) to score at least Proficient in mathematics?
- Why are there achievement gaps?
- What am I doing in my classroom to promote learning that's most effective?
- What am I doing in my classroom to promote learning that's least effective?
- How well do I know my curriculum standards?
- Am I teaching to the standards?
- What do I do when students don't master the standards?
- What can I do to improve parent participation?

Involve other stakeholders in the formulation of the key questions, to ensure wide coverage of perceptions. One value of this analysis of perceptual data is to dispel commonly held assumptions about what causes poor student achievement. For example, a focus discussion may show that teachers commonly believe that eighth-grade students from certain low-income housing areas have poor attendance or poor achievement levels. After analyzing the eighth-grade data in the School Numeracy Profile, they find no correlation between income and poor attendance or poor performance for those students.

Changing the Perception of AP Participation...Imagine That

Students selected for enrollment in an AP English Literature class by high grades and teacher recommendation continued to score average to below on the annual AP exam. Finally, the AP teacher with the support of the school guidance counselor, identified additional students for the upcoming year by looking at high ACT, PSAT, or SAT verbal scores. The teacher interviewed each of the new students during the summer and informed parents and students of teacher and peer support systems available to students who struggle. Throughout the academic year, the teacher continued with periodic progress meetings. Compared with the previous year, twice as many students received a score of 3 on the AP exam, several more students achieved a 4, and, for the first time, four students achieved the highest rating of 5.

Summative data

Summative data include the annual state standardized mathematics assessment test mastery and nonmastery group report results. Student group scores are reported by grade level and by subgroup. Since group reports give data for a single testing year, the team should collect group reports from 2002 to the present and organize them into tables or graphs for easy reference. Tables 3-1, 3-2, 3-3, and 3-4 represent several examples of summative trend data, which are explained in sample tables with analysis hints, analysis questions, and numeracy team discussion items that will help you organize and represent your own school data.

For high schools, the team should also collect data from college entrance or AP mathematics exams. If you have a local university or community college, request several years' mathematics placement exam results of freshmen from your school.

TABLE 3-1

Summative Trend Data 3–5 Years
Schoolwide Mathematics Scores
% Proficient or Above

GRADE	2002	2003	2004	2005
5	57↘	61	63	60
6	51	59↘	62	64
7	55	56	56↘	63
8	50	56	58	58

Analysis hint: The 2002 fifth graders became eighth graders in 2005 (follow the diagonal).

Analysis questions:

- What percentage of eighth graders were Proficient or above in 2005?
- Did the eighth graders' scores improve when compared with the previous year's scores (follow the diagonal up and left)?

Numeracy team discussion: Do your students' mathematics test scores improve as time in the school's educational program increases? What instructional strategies, grouping by grade-level teams or departmental teams, and intervention activities may be employed?

Since the numeracy team is in search of specific content standards not mastered and effective instructional strategies or interventions that the grade-level or content teachers might be able to employ, your team now needs to investigate what student groups are Proficient in mathematics assessment skill areas and what student groups are not. Further analyses of student performance data can be found by analyzing the student group report. This is information that your district reports to the state as required by federal law and this report is, in many cases, also sent to your school. If you do not receive data by subgroup, request it from the district office before compiling it on site. Compiling the data in a format such as in Table 3-2 enables the team to look at mathematics performance levels by student groups.

TABLE 3-2

Summative Test Scores by Student Grade and Group

Student Group Grade 10	2002				2003				2004				2005			
Performance →	BB	B	Pro	Adv	BB	B	Pro	Adv	BB	B	Pro	Adv	BB	B	Pro	Adv
Asian	27%	46%	27%	0	27%	18%	46%	9%	13%	27%	47%	13%	6%	33%	43%	18%
Black	45%	37%	18%	0	29%	21%	36%	14%	31%	28%	16%	25%	19%	20%	36%	25%
White	27%	55%	13%	5%	22%	62%	11%	5%	21%	49%	20%	10%	13%	52%	23%	12%
Hispanic	61%	17%	22%	0	48%	36%	16%	0	29%	36%	26%	9%	18%	51%	22%	9%
Male	34%	26%	28%	12%	25%	30%	30%	15%	20%	27%	35%	18%	15%	23%	40%	22%
Female	30%	42%	20%	8%	24%	41%	25%	10%	18%	42%	30%	10%	15%	35%	35%	15%
Economically disadvantaged	45%	40%	10%	5%	42%	35%	15%	8%	38%	35%	20%	7%	35%	30%	25%	10%
Economically advantaged	30%	40%	25%	5%	25%	35%	30%	10%	18%	30%	25%	27%	15%	25%	30%	30%
Special education	65%	35%	0%	0%	62%	38%	0%	0%	58%	40%	2%	0%	46%	38%	16%	0%
English language learners	40%	55%	5%	0%	35%	65%	0%	0%	30%	55%	13%	2%	33%	51%	11%	5%

BB = Below Basic   B = Basic   Pro = Proficient   Adv = Advanced

Analysis hint: Check to see that all measurable subgroups in your school are represented in the table. Be sure you look at and record 3–5 years of school profile data. Cluster groups from the table (ethnic, gender, economics, educational program).

Analysis questions:

■ What ethnic group has the highest percentage of students who are Proficient and above for 2005?

■ In which groups has the percentage of BB (Below Basic) students decreased from 2002 to 2005?

■ In what groups have the percentage of students that are Proficient and above increased from 2002 to 2005?

Charting the improvement of scores by subgroups may be more clearly seen when represented in a line graph or bar graph. In the sample table below, the percentage of student ethnic groups scoring Proficient or above is shown. (In calculating the percentage of students scoring at Proficient or above, add the percentage Proficient and percentage Advanced in the same year.) The resulting line graph answers the following analyses question more clearly: Has the percentage of student groups scoring at Proficient or above, increased over the trend years?

FIGURE 3-1

Summary Table for Graph from Table 3-2—Groups Proficient or Above

% of Ethnic Students Proficient or Above

Ethnic Group	2002	2003	2004	2005
Asian	27	55	60	61
Black	18	50	41	61
White	18	16	30	35
Hispanic	22	16	35	31

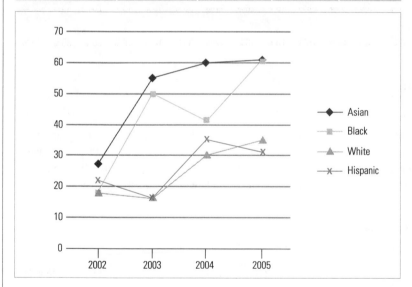

Analysis hint: It might be beneficial to graph all of the student groups scoring at Proficient or above and also to graph all student groups scoring at basic and below. These graphs may facilitate answers to the analysis questions and numeracy team discussions identified for Table 3-2 and the line graph.

Numeracy team discussion: What student groups have or have not improved each year? What grade-level or mathematics initiatives have been implemented with various subgroups and has the percentage of Proficient and above increased in these groups? What groups are NOT achieving Proficient (BB + B)? What groups need to be targeted for instructional support?

Table 3-3 shows the results of an item analysis of the mathematics assessment skill areas and the student group (grade 7) scoring below Proficient.

TABLE 3-3
Grade-Level Mathematics Performance Summary
Mathematics Assessment Content Standard Skill
Standardized Mathematics Group Profile, Part I: 48 questions

MATHEMATICS—GRADE 7		
(48 questions)		
Skill	No. of Questions	% of Students Below Proficient
Numbers and Number Relations	5	40
Measurement	6	45
Statistics	5	25
Number Systems/Number Theory	5	30
Algebra	5	15
Probability	6	38
Patterns & Functions	5	35
Geometry	5	20
Problem-Solving Strategies	6	55

Analysis hint: Note the following information in Table 3-3: 40% of all seventh-grade students scored less than Proficient in Numbers and Number Relations; 45% of all seventh graders scored less than Proficient in Measurement; 25% of all seventh graders scored less than Proficient in Statistics; 30% of all seventh graders scored less than Proficient in Number Systems/Number Theory.

Analysis questions:

- What mathematics skill areas need greatest reinforcement?
- Has the team matched the mathematics skill assessment areas with the grade-level curriculum standards?

Numeracy team discussion: Focus on the areas of greatest need. Most seventh graders need problem-solving examples (55% below Proficient) for practice. Has the team identified the mathematics grade-level curriculum standards that are not mastered? (This alignment has already been done by most states and/or districts.) Has the team identified the cross-content mathematics standards that also were not mastered in the mathematics skill areas of the profile? For ease in identifying what skill areas need highest instructional priority, rank the skill areas from the highest area of nonmastery to the lowest, as in Table 3-4.

TABLE 3-4

Grade-Level Mathematics Performance Summary

Ranked Standardized Mathematics Group Profile, Part I: 48 questions

MATHEMATICS—GRADE 7			
(48 questions)			
Skill	No. of Questions	% of Students Below Proficient	Priority Ranking
Problem-Solving Strategies	6	55	1
Measurement	6	45	2
Number & Number Relations	5	40	3
Probability	6	38	4
Patterns & Functions	5	35	5
Number Systems/Number Theory	5	30	6
Statistics	5	25	7
Geometry	5	20	8
Algebra	5	15	9

Analysis questions:

- How many priority areas will be emphasized and what is the timeline?
- How many skills will be reinforced during each grading period?
- What content standards are embedded in each skill area?
- When will the skills be evaluated by the benchmark exam?
- What skills can be reinforced in mathematics classes?
- What activities can reinforce needed mathematics skills in other content classes?
- What interdisciplinary projects and activities will provide practice in the priority skill areas?

Numeracy team discussion: Seventh-grade teachers should spend about 9 weeks teaching/ reinforcing skills ranked 1 to 4 in Table 3-4: Problem-Solving Strategies, Measurement, Numbers and Number Relations, and Probability. The benchmark exam will be taken in week 10. For example:

Mathematics class reinforcement—Sample lessons in Problem solving can be found in the seventh-grade mathematics text as follows: Measurement, pp. 26–27; Probability & Statistics, pp. 30–35; Number systems & Relations, pp. 40–45; problem-solving strategies, pp. 50–60. Content classes—A sample interdisciplinary project will be identified for implementation by grade-level teams.

The team should identify performance objectives, outcomes, timelines, and resources for content-area teachers and ask teachers to maintain a mastery log containing the following items: performance, outcome, time, resources, test score.

Formative data

Formative data are collected throughout the year but are also summarized at the close of the school year. Compile these data by grade level and by subgroup. These data include mathematics grades, local school benchmark exams, interim mathematics exam results, mathematics final exam grades, etc.

Demographic data

Demographic data give a summary of the characteristics of the school population. They describe the common characteristics and variations of the school's subgroups. The number of students in each of the 10 federal reporting subgroups, the number in each grade level, the number of students who receive free and reduced-price meals in each grade, the number of students completing mathematics courses in each grade level by subgroup, school absences and tardies in each group, ages, number of students retained in each grade level by subgroup, etc.

The following is a sample of schoolwide demographic data points that can be effectively summarized in table form:

- Population—show across 5 years
- Attendance—show monthly for 1 year by subgroups
- Suspensions—show number of days missed/student group test scores
- Benchmark testing—show group score gains over 1 year
- Student subgroups—show group size, scores over 4 years
- Educational program (gifted and talented, special education, ELL, bilingual, etc.)—show population.

Table 3-5 represents a performance data sample using one of the demographic data points. In this sample, mathematics performance is summarized by economic status as measured by the percentage of students eligible for free and reduced-price meals and those eligible for paid meals.

TABLE 3-5

Mathematics Scores by Economic Status

Grade	Economic Status	Performance	2003		2004		2005	
			No.	%	No.	%	No.	%
9	Free/Reduced-Price Meals	Below Standard	30	50	25	42	20	33
		Meets Standard	20	33	25	42	28	47
		Advanced	10	17	10	17	12	20
	Paid	Below Standard	10	25	10	25	8	20
		Meets Standard	25	62	26	65	25	62
		Advanced	5	13	4	10	7	18
10	Free/Reduced-Price Meals	Below Standard	30	67	25	55	20	44
		Meets Standard	10	22	15	33	20	44
		Advanced	5	11	5	11	5	11
	Paid	Below Standard	15	27	13	24	10	18
		Meets Standard	30	55	30	55	33	60
		Advanced	10	18	12	22	12	22

Analysis hint: Note that 67% of the students in grade 9 who receive free and reduced-price lunch in 2005 are Proficient or above (47% + 20%), while 33 % are not; 80% of the grade 9 paid-lunch students in 2005 are Proficient or above (62% + 18%).

Note: rounded total may be between 99 and 101.

Analysis questions:

- Did the percentage of Below Standard students decrease between 2003 and 2005?

- Did the percentage of Proficient students increase between 2003 and 2005?

- Did the percentage of the Proficient and above students in all groups increase between 2003 and 2005?

Numeracy team discussions: Who were the students in the Below Standard group in 2005? Are these students also identified in the poor attendance or suspension group? If an early-morning or after-school intervention is planned, will some students need additional resources to participate (costs for transportation, supplemental materials, etc.)? What specific interventions are possible for small-group or individual instruction?

Creating the School Numeracy Profile

The School Numeracy Profile is informed by analysis of the data collected in each of the four types of assessment data. To truly create a culture of numeracy, staff should focus first on collecting perceptual data in focus groups and then on the analysis of summative, formative, and demographic group data. See Appendix 6 for a profile template.

The School Numeracy Profile is a document that should be provided to all staff members for study and discussion. Teachers should be assisted in analyzing variables, discussing correlations, and utilizing the data to plan long-term mathematics improvement strategies. This document can also be used to help frame the discussion about your teachers' professional development needs as you build capacity for mathematics improvement within the school culture.

Gathering the data and finding the answers to the questions below should reveal the areas of student nonmastery that need to be addressed both by individual mathematics classes and in content-area classrooms:

- What are the mathematics concepts that students have mastered at each grade level?
- What are the mathematics concepts that students have not effectively mastered?
- What mathematics standards are effectively mastered after completing the grade-level mathematics course?
- How are specific groups of students performing in mathematics?
- How has attendance affected mathematics performance?
- What are the longitudinal trends for mathematics mastery for groups of students in your school?
- How does completion of specific mathematics courses affect mastery of mathematics concepts?
- Are additional data needed to successfully answer these questions?
- How can feeder elementary schools and middle schools support student areas of mastery and nonmastery?

The school staff can focus the data analysis by developing key analysis questions. The numeracy team, supported by its findings in asking and answering key questions, should complete the school profile and identify the mathematics concepts to be the instructional focus during the upcoming school year. Answering key questions will not only help to focus what concepts have or have not been mastered but will also identify the appropriate grade-level content classes where mathematics skills may be met and the curriculum standards addressed by the grade-level mathematics curriculum. Instructional areas where staff members seem unsure or underprepared are areas to be strongly supported by professional development.

FIGURE 3-2

Four types of assessment data formulating the School Numeracy Profile

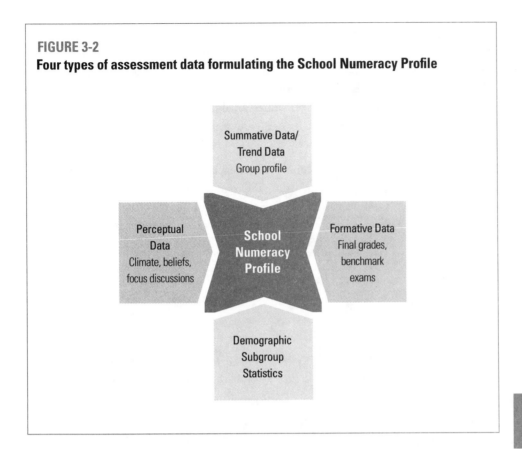

Analyzing Data to Complete the Personal Plan for Mathematics Proficiency

The numeracy team should collect current data to build a Personal Plan for Mathematics Proficiency (PP4MP) for each student. In comparison with the School Numeracy Profile and its analyses of student group data, the PP4MP compiles data to identify the mathematics concepts mastered and not mastered by individual students. To complete this individual profile, the numeracy team collect a variety of data from many school sources. The team will disaggregate multiple sources of student data, looking at grade-level mathematics areas of mastery and nonmastery for each student.

The PP4MP is completed by the student or team member and is based on the attitudes about mathematics achievement from the student focus interview and from the mastery skills information data collected from school sources and the assessment student profile data. Establish a process for the completion of the personal plan by each student. It might be completed by the student or teacher in advisory or by a counselor or mentor in a student interview session. If the plan is completed by team members or teachers, provide time for student and teacher discussion and review.

Numeracy team data analysis will provide individual student data to complete the PP4MP. This plan is a summary of the mathematics content standards mastered or not mastered by each student, and data analysis should go deeper than standardized data. Members of the numeracy team are responsible for analyzing multiple forms of assessment as well as school and teacher data to identify the mathematics skills accomplished

■ Suggested data sources for the PP4MP are student results on state assessments, district assessment exams, school benchmark tests, diagnostic assessments, classroom assessments, and mathematics final exams, mathematics advisory grades; attendance information; and records from the perception focus discussion.

and those needing reinforcement. The PP4MP identifies the learning needs of each student so that staff members and the student can plan for progress. As with the school profile, the PP4MP comes from analyzing and carefully representing four types of schoolwide data. Principals who have had little or no experience analyzing this type of individual student data might consider professional development in this area through district or state resources.

Perceptual data

Perceptual data reflect the opinions and views of each student about his or her own mathematics mastery and ability. Preceding the examination of the data compiled for the PP4MP, students should participate in a focus discussion regarding their perception about what mathematics concepts they think they have mastered, trouble areas, and why they have achieved proficiency or why they have not achieved proficiency in mathematics on assessment tests. These focused discussions are preferably completed in individual or small groups. The numeracy team or staff should compile pertinent discussion questions and identify teacher or counselor interviewers to ask and record the answers to key questions such as:

- Are you good at mathematics? Why do you think that?
- In which mathematics courses have you experienced the most success?
- Where have you had the least success in mathematics? Why do you think that is?
- How many hours a week do you study mathematics?

Be sure to include other stakeholders in the formulation of these key questions to give a broader perspective. Many times the value of this perception analysis may be to dispel commonly held assumptions about poor achievement. For example, many mathematics students commonly believe that fractions or geometry are areas of poor achievement and find, after analyzing the data compiled for the PP4MP, that they have sufficient skills in those areas to be scored as Proficient. Students who believe that mathematics is not related to practice and preparation may discover that too few hours are spent studying mathematics to be successful. Students may be presented with an opportunity to see the inconsistency between their common beliefs and the data.

Summative data

Summative data include the annual student profiles provided by the standardized mathematics assessment test results. These individual student reports are traditionally provided by the state or district. If profiles are not provided, they can be requested from the district or state or they can be compiled from the scored test item analysis of each student. Scores from benchmark mathematics exams, college entrance mathematics exams, or AP mathematics exams should also be included. Table 3-6 is a sample individual student profile provided by the state.

TABLE 3-6
Sample Individual Mathematics State Performance Report

Mathematics Assessment by Individual and Content Skill

MATHEMATICS—GRADE 9 Scaled Score = 344		
Skill	**No. of Questions**	**Number Correct**
Numbers and Number Relations	9	6
Geometry and Measurement	12	9
Patterns & Functions	6	6
Algebra	7	7
Probability and Statistics	7	4
Computation and Estimation	8	5
Problem-Solving Strategies	11	7

Analysis hints: Identify the content standards that are tested in each of the skill areas. Note the mastered skills and the skills that need reinforcement. Find the scale score range of the next performance level and determine how many points this student needs to score at the next performance level.

Analysis question: What reinforcement activities can be accomplished by this student either individually with learning packets or in small groups with instruction that will improve mastery in the identified skill area?

Numeracy team/teacher discussion: What skills will be addressed in mathematics classes or what skills can be reinforced in content classes? How many classroom students need reinforcement in the same skills areas? What skills can be reinforced individually, in small groups or in pull-out groups?

Chapter 3: Analyzing Data for Schoolwide and Individual Student Improvement

Formative data

Formative data are classroom and school data collected throughout the year and used to inform instruction decisions. At the beginning of the year, compile these data by examining grades from previous marking periods, unit tests, mathematics exam grades, and final exams in mathematics. These data include local school benchmark mathematics exam results. Establish a plan to store and display the formative data and an update process throughout the school year that identifies current mastered and nonmastered skills so that each student and teacher can monitor mastery changes.

Demographic data

Demographic data describe the common characteristics and variations of each student in the population, the number of mathematics courses completed in each grade level, grades, school absences and tardies, etc.

Creating the Personal Plan for Mathematics Proficiency

The PP4MP is a four-part document that is informed by the data collected in each of the four categories. To truly create a culture of numeracy, the initial focus for the PP4MP should be on recording the perceptual data followed by analyzing the data compiled for the other three types. See Appendix 7 for a PP4MP template.

The mastered and nonmastered mathematics skills/concepts should be presented for discussion by the numeracy team, grade level, and/or departmental teams. They will inform the content of the schoolwide Numeracy Improvement Plan and provide information about meeting standards in both the grade-level mathematics course and in the interdisciplinary mathematics skills in content courses. The student plan compiled from assessment data will provide information for teachers, parents, and students.

Effective use of the student personal plan will provide factual information to make appropriate mathematics instructional decisions. By reviewing the collective personal plans in a classroom, the teacher will be able to make grouping and reinforcement decisions to address mathematics deficiencies. Utilizing formative assessment data throughout the year will update instructional decisions and focus reinforcement where it is currently needed. (See figure 3-2.)

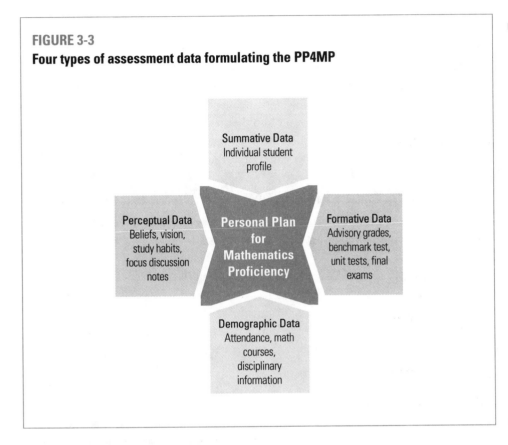

FIGURE 3-3

Four types of assessment data formulating the PP4MP

Summative Data
Individual student profile

Perceptual Data
Beliefs, vision, study habits, focus discussion notes

Personal Plan for Mathematics Proficiency

Formative Data
Advisory grades, benchmark test, unit tests, final exams

Demographic Data
Attendance, math courses, disciplinary information

■ Analyze the School Numeracy Profile built from mathematics assessment data and school and classroom assessments to determine the specific mathematics learning needs of student groups. Group and regroup to address the nonmastered skills identified for each student in the Personal Plans for Mathematics Proficiency.
■ Initiate strategies to "plug the gaps!"

Chapter 3: Analyzing Data for Schoolwide and Individual Student Improvement

Informing the School Improvement Planning Process

Your staff and stakeholders must understand that testing will focus the school on what it is doing right as well as what needs to be improved.

A successful schoolwide improvement initiative in mathematics (i.e., Numeracy Improvement Plan), depends on authentic interpretation of school information in two major areas: rigor and mastery in mathematics courses and rigor and mastery in cross-content reinforcement of mathematics skills.

Rigor in mathematics courses

The numeracy team should analyze mathematics mastery based on the number of mathematics courses students have completed. This provides an environment to ask if proficiency improves with successful completion of yearly mathematics classes. This process will inform additional key questions:

- Is there equity of participation in all school mathematics courses?
- Does completion of a rigorous mathematics course in sequence improve mathematics proficiency for all students?

Table 3-7 is a sample of the percentage of students from each school subgroup enrolled in two secondary mathematics courses. Your team should complete these demographics for all school mathematics courses. Underrepresented groups in each course are identified by shading, and equity of participation can easily be seen. Table 3-8 is a sample of the data to be collected and summarized by the team, showing how students in each mathematics course scored on the mathematics section of the most recent state exam. In a large school with a large number of mathematics courses, a random sample of students can be utilized; or, where there are many sections of the same course, a random selection of one or two sections can be used.

TABLE 3-7

Mathematics Class Demographics

2006–07 School Year	Total	Male	Female	Free/ Reduce	Paid	Black	White	Hispanic	Asian	Special Education
School	N=600 100%	N=280 47%	N=320 53%	N=175 29%	N=425 71%	N=80 13%	N=270 45%	N=200 33%	N=50 8%	N=5 1%
Calculus	N=30 100%	N=20 **67%**	N=10 33%	N=1 3%	N=29 **97%**	N=2 7%	N=14% **47%**	N=2 7%	N=12 **40%**	N=0 0%
Pre-Calculus	N=60 100%	N=40 **67%**	N=20 33%	N=5 8%	N=55 **92%**	N=3 5%	N=35 **58%**	N=5 8%	N=17 **28%**	N=0 0%

Boxed numbers = underrepresented
Bolded numbers = overrepresented

Analysis hint: Shading and bolding will help you identify overrepresentation and underrepresentation at a glance so that time may be better spent on identifying strategies for class balancing. The team should complete the table for every mathematics course.

Analysis questions:

- Is there equity of participation in my classes? (See White students in Calculus.)
- Have those student groups identified as below Proficient completed sequentially challenging mathematics courses?

Numeracy team discussion: The demographics in your school's mathematics classes should parallel the demographics in your school. The numeracy team may need to identify recruitment strategies in your plan to increase the number of underrepresented subgroups in mathematics course electives. Traditionally, finding the same ethnic and economic demographics across the mathematics curriculum is a challenge and certainly may need a concerted effort by the team, counselors, and teachers.

TABLE 3-8
Performance Levels by Mathematics Course

Course	9th Grade	2005	10th Grade	2005	Level
	No.	%	No.	%	
Pre-Algebra	50	70	10	60	Nearing
		20		40	Proficient
		10			Advanced
Algebra	100	40	20	50	Nearing
		50		40	Proficient
		10		10	Advanced
Geometry	40	30	90	30	Nearing
		50		50	Proficient
		20		20	Advanced
Int. Algebra	10	5	25	10	Nearing
		60		50	Proficient
		35		40	Advanced
Pre-Calculus	0	0	5	0	Nearing
		0		70	Proficient
		0		30	Advanced
Calculus	0	0	0	0	Nearing
		0		0	Proficient
		0		0	Advanced
TOTAL	200		150		

Analysis hint: Depending on the number of students enrolled in your school and the availability of prepared assessment profiles, your team may need to randomly select the assessment scores of a subset of students in each grade.

Analysis questions:

- What are the demographic data of the student groups nearing Proficient (include points such as attendance, mathematics grades, etc.)?
- What are the demographics of the student groups that are Proficient or above?
- Do students who stay in rigorous mathematics courses continue to score higher than students who do not?

Numeracy team discussion: Does mathematics mastery (percentage of Proficient or above) improve as students complete more rigorous mathematics courses? Look at the demographics of each group and identify the variables that affect their achievement.

Crosscontent mathematics skills

Mathematics skills are embedded in content areas and are identified in the course curriculum content standards. It is the challenge of the numeracy team to identify nonmastered mathematics concepts and devise interdisciplinary and disciplinary instructional activities to reinforce the mastery of these skills. The designed activities should be enriched by real-life examples utilizing technology and the problem-solving process.

Determining the schoolwide attitudes/perceptions, strengths, and weaknesses of the mathematics program in the process of developing the School Numeracy Profile and the strengths and weaknesses of individual students in the Personal Plan for Mathematics Proficiency make them powerful tools in designing schoolwide initiatives that will improve mathematics instruction for *every* student. Changing your school to a culture that supports numeracy and encourages engagement of all students and faculty members in mathematics mastery means that *test* does not become just another "four-letter word" but has the power to improve student performance.

Simulated Numeracy Discussion

Participants: Numeracy team with the grade-level or departmental team(s).

Materials: Content standards and curriculum, School Numeracy Profile with nonmastered mathematics standards identified.

Key questions: What real-life situation exemplifies the mathematics concept that many students have not mastered? What interdisciplinary mathematics skills can be taught in those activities and/or projects? What mathematics skills can be reinforced in content classrooms? What problem-solving skills and technology skills can be utilized in solving or simulating the solution to the instructional activity?

Discussion: If 10th-grade students have not mastered graphics representation and data summarization concepts, perhaps social studies teachers can integrate graphs and mapping exercises into classroom instruction. Science teachers can ask students to summarize laboratory data in tables and graph the results. English teachers can demonstrate the use of graphic organizers. Computer teachers can teach Excel pie and bar graph representation. Simultaneously, the grade-level mathematics class can teach Cartesian coordinate systems, functions, and graphing. Each rigorous content-area teacher can reinforce the identified mathematics standard in the classroom as well as work within his/her team to design real-life cross-curricular projects and activities that provide students with opportunities to problem solve in groups, utilize technology, and practice nonmastered mathematics concepts.

As you and your numeracy team begin to evaluate assessment data, plan strategies for interventions or supports, and develop the schoolwide Numeracy Improvement Plan, use the focus discussion in Figure 3-4 as the framework for the plan.

FIGURE 3-4
Focus Discussion Framework

COMPONENT	KEY QUESTIONS
School Numeracy Profile	What are the math concepts that are effectively mastered by grade-level students?
	What percentage of students are enrolled in sequentially difficult mathematics courses each year?
	How will you address the specific mathematics needs of all students?
	How can all content teachers contribute to improving mathematics mastery?

OUTCOMES
Determining strengths and weaknesses of the mathematics program identified in the School Numeracy Profile can give the numeracy team an opportunity to plan interdisciplinary activities and projects that will support and reinforce needed mathematics skills/concepts both in mathematics classes and in content classes.

COMPONENT	KEY QUESTIONS
Professional Development Needs	Do teachers have the knowledge to identify and develop instructional materials that utilize mathematics skills as a tool?
	Can teachers utilize data to differentiate instruction?
	Can teachers identify real-life activities and interdisciplinary projects that utilize problem-solving skills, mathematics skills, and technology skills?
	Have teachers had an opportunity to identify their own professional development needs?

OUTCOMES
Since effective teaching of students with diverse mathematics preparation relies heavily on a repertoire of instructional strategies, the numeracy team may need to address the acquisition of these skills in the plan for the professional development of the staff. Facilitating classroom team activities, integrating technology, and developing higher-level thinking skills may be additional needs. In addition, the numeracy team needs to provide aggregate data to the feeder schools to improve and reinforce the mathematics skills of transition students. Perhaps a joint staff development can be planned with school and feeder-school faculty. Long-term nonmastery trend data should be addressed in collaboration with feeder-school faculty. Strategies for building effective collaborative leadership teams may also need to be addressed in the professional development plan.

COMPONENT	KEY QUESTIONS
Strategies to Close the Achievement Gap	Has each teacher received the PP4MP for each student in the classroom?
	How many students need to be targeted for intervention or support in each mathematics content skill area?
	Should reinforcement occur individually or in small groups?
	Which interdisciplinary groups of teachers may address specific topics in content classrooms or in pull-out groups?
	Are additional resources needed to "level the playing field" for specific subgroups?

OUTCOMES

As more and more teachers are facilitating classrooms with increased diversity, "what we teach and how we teach it" is a critical issue in addressing the achievement gap for every student. Closing the achievement gap for students means that teachers must deliver instruction to students with a variety of learning styles, differing socioeconomic backgrounds, and a disparity of prior knowledge. Requiring mathematics proficiency of all students will require an individualized look by all staff members at what each student has mastered and what needs to be mastered as identified in the Personal Plan for Mathematics Proficiency and what learning style is most effective with individual students?

COMPONENT	KEY QUESTIONS
Personal Plan for Mathematics Mastery	Has each student set goals based on individual skill profiles?
	Are students given opportunities for practice and support?
	Are students given ample opportunities during the year to demonstrate growth on benchmark tests?
	Are personal plans revised/updated throughout the year?
	Has the teacher compiled a classroom profile using the student PP4MPs?
	Are teachers addressing the specific learning needs of the students in large or small groups within their classes?
	Are content-specific instructional activities and resources available to teachers, parents, and students?
	Are students encouraged to continue mathematics in sequence each year?

OUTCOMES

The personal plan completed with the data elements previously described must be analyzed by each teacher and each teacher team responsible for that student's learning. In standardized assessments, students are given a grade equivalent or a criterion standard with specific content strengths and weaknesses identified. Your school team must examine and discuss the data to identify individual students who are scoring below grade level or below Proficient in mathematics and analyze the particular skills that a student needs to master to improve mathematics competency and identify the effective learning styles of the student. That means, to fully and properly evaluate student strengths and weaknesses in mathematics, the team must use valid and reliable benchmark exams given several times during the school year with individual student data results. The numeracy team should schedule several team meetings during the school year to evaluate the progress of individual students toward mathematics mastery and revise the school improvement support plan as needed for individual students. Benchmark testing can inform the monitoring process by determining the success of embedded classroom activities in meeting mathematics standards.

COMPONENT	KEY QUESTIONS
Rigorous Mathematics Instruction	Have your mathematics teachers worked to design common course objectives, assessments, and activities to reinforce nonmastered skills in the personal plans?
	Have your content-area teachers, working closely with the mathematics resource person/department chair (or designee), worked to design specific content activities that support the mathematics learning needs of their content areas?
	Has the numeracy team collected commercial, district, or teacher-prepared best-practice mathematics activities for embedded classroom instruction?
	Does every teacher know and understand what the data reveal about the mathematics content mastery of each student within his or her classroom?

OUTCOMES
Standardized tests can serve as a baseline to determine which skills have not been mastered by your students. Many state and local assessments can identify specific areas of student mastery and nonmastery aligned to state or local mathematics content standards. Identify what mathematics skills/content standards are taught in each course and plot a sequential skills progression for each student matriculating in your school. A review of the skills aggregate of the PP4MP can identify teaming and instructional strategies.

Understanding the four types of data, what local school data to collect, the procedures for analyzing this data, and the representation of data in table and graphic form are essential to the process of identifying actions and initiatives for your schoolwide Numeracy Improvement Plan. The School Numeracy Profile and the Personal Plans for Mathematics Proficiency are documents that will inform the design, focus, and training needed to make your plan successful. Remember that accurately interpreting and analyzing data will serve as the foundations for school improvement decisions. Asking key questions and seeking answers verified by data are important techniques for the numeracy team that verifies what the school is doing right and identifies what the school needs to improve. All stakeholders must study the techniques for data representation from this chapter to accurately set learning goals and track student progress. It is now time to make *data* your favorite "four-letter word."

Schoolwide Data

_____ Assist the numeracy team in examining long-term trend data (three to five years) to identify school areas of strength/weakness, mastery/nonmastery

_____ Discuss the results with the numeracy team, departments, grade-level teachers, and other staff members

_____ Establish a format for the School Numeracy Profile

_____ Use the inquiry method (key questions) to compile data for the School Numeracy Profile

_____ Include the following types of data in the School Numeracy Profile:

    _____ Perceptual data

    _____ Summative data

    _____ Formative data

    _____ Demographic data.

Student Data

_____ Assist the numeracy team in examining multiple sources of student data to reveal areas of individual student mastery to be addressed

_____ Discuss the results with the numeracy team, departments, grade-level teachers and other staff members

_____ Establish a format and a process for completion of the Personal Plan for Mathematics Proficiency based on data collected on each student

_____ Use the inquiry method (key questions) to compile data for the student plan

_____ Include the following types of data in the PP4MP:

    _____ Perceptual data

    _____ Demographic data

    _____ Formative data

    _____ Summative data

_____ Establish methods for parent involvement and communication

_____ Establish a process to monitor and evaluate mastery on an ongoing basis.

Numeracy Improvement Plan

_____ Use the data to inform the content of the plan

_____ Identify professional development needs

_____ Devise strategies to close the achievement gaps

_____ Formulate objectives and activities based on each student's PP4MP

_____ Employ methods to ensure that all mathematics and other content-area teachers are engaged in rigorous mathematics instruction

_____ Plot mathematics skills by sequential courses in both math and content areas

_____ Establish a process to monitor and evaluate plan implementation.

4 Promoting a Rigorous Schoolwide Numeracy Curriculum

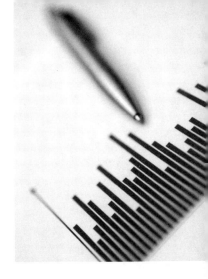

They were all sitting around one table. Mathematics faculty from two middle schools, two high schools, a community college, and the local university. As they talked, a startling fact suddenly hit them: every one of their institutions offered the exact same course...at one level, that course—Algebra 1—was taught to the most advanced students, while at another level it was taught to the least advanced students."

—*Kati Haycock, Executive Director, The Education Trust*

The goal of the Numeracy Improvement Plan, spearheaded by the principal and the numeracy team, is both to provide a rigorous mathematics curriculum for all students in every secondary grade and to implement rigorous mathematics activities embedded with the reasoning skills and concepts of the content area. The mathematics activities designed for every classroom support the skills and knowledge of the content area and utilize mathematics and technology as problem-solving tools. Ensuring continuous progress toward the goal of rigorous mathematics instruction in all classrooms requires the implementation of the three core areas in the *Breaking Ranks™* publications:

- Collaborative leadership
- Personalization
- Curriculum, instruction, and assessment.

The recommendations from these core areas are informed by school data with the instructional support of the numeracy team and the persistent monitoring of the effectiveness of the effort through classroom visitations, targeted staff development, and purposeful teacher evaluations. Perhaps the initiatives identified in the Numeracy Improvement Plan, informed by the School Numeracy Profile and the Personal Plan for Mathematics Proficiency, may even eliminate the need for the course duplication for students described above by Kati Haycock.

How Can Rigorous Mathematics Curriculum Serve as a Catalyst for Change in Secondary Schools?

Public policy studies reveal a direct correlation between schooling and labor market success; further, the *level* of mathematics courses that a student takes is even more important. Rose and Betts (2001) found a strong relationship between advanced mathematics course completion in high school and higher labor market earnings 10 years after graduation. Selecting a rigorous curriculum that requires completing annual mathematics courses in elementary through high school leads to increased student success at the university level and in the labor market.

What a principal can do to support a rigorous mathematics program:

- Analyze schoolwide mathematics data to complete school and individual profiles
- Engage faculty in discussions about building consensus for evaluating student work
- Improve mathematics instruction
- Develop interdisciplinary, high-performing, collaborative teacher teams
- Utilize stakeholders and data to develop a Numeracy Improvement Plan
- Provide opportunities for teacher growth
- Engage parents and community members
- Commit resources for mathematics improvement
- Provide support programs for students and parents
- Monitor good classroom instruction
- Schedule planning opportunities for teachers
- Raise expectation levels
- Encourage student enrollment in mathematics each year
- Identify and/or provide summer learning opportunities in mathematics for teachers and students.

The principal has a unique opportunity to shape the academic environment for *every* student and so must provide a sequenced, standards-based, rigorous mathematics curriculum. Students are expected to complete a set of required mathematics courses and Carnegie credits for promotion or to receive a high school diploma, but often they are not encouraged to complete rigorous mathematics courses every year throughout middle level and high school. When more students are challenged to complete accelerated mathematics courses, school culture undergoes an immediate and substantial change. *Raise the bar; raise the scrutiny on the mathematics program.* Students need the encouragement and support of the whole school community as they learn about the postsecondary opportunities that increased mathematics electives will afford them and as they stretch to meet these higher expectations. All school stakeholders must understand that numeracy is a set of skills that must be pursued every day, every year.

The faculty members at Arroyo High School in El Monte, CA, understand the strong relationship between adult expectations and student outcomes. The faculty members have demonstrated that when adults believe that students can be successful in an academically rigorous environment, students achieve. Like at Arroyo, students throughout the country have shown that when adults demonstrate belief in their abilities, students are willing to accept more difficult challenges. In fact, when adults "share their passion for learning with students, students become passionate learners themselves" (Mero, Hartzman, and Boone, 2005, p. 53).

Many students haven't been challenged with the necessary accelerated mathematics electives before graduation. Often, these mathematics electives are seen as applicable only to those students expressing a desire to attend college. Algebra is considered a "glass ceiling" because the limitations imposed by its nonmastery are not immediately apparent. In the local, national, and international job markets in which our young people will compete, their selection for many high-paying technical positions may be improved by completing the accelerated mathematics electives once thought only to benefit university-bound students. Adults must be actively engaged in encouraging young people to enroll in challenging mathematics courses.

High expectations for every student should provide opportunities for more challenging mathematics electives for the majority of your students. The minimum mathematics elective for all students must be raised to Intermediate Algebra with Trigonometry as a schoolwide mathematics minimum. But requiring accelerated mathematics electives of the majority of the student body without successful teacher preparation; an aligned curriculum in the feeder schools; community education; and support programs for students with tutoring, mentoring, and supplemental services may lead to increased student and parent frustration. Without the thoughtful planning and preparation of the numeracy team, the best intentions may go unrewarded. Students can only become more marketable through increased mathematics instruction if they are encouraged and successfully supported.

Rigorous Instruction in the Mathematics Classroom

The school administrator must provide many opportunities for the mathematics faculty to begin the conversation about mathematics rigor and what it looks like in the classroom. What are teacher behaviors in this rigorous classroom? What are student behaviors in this rigorous classroom? What are the instructional goals of this rigorous curriculum? These discussions about rigor, framed and developed in Chapter 1 (see also Appendix 3), should lead the mathematics faculty to focus on the three requisite areas of an effective mathematics classroom:

- **High curriculum standards** include collaborative planning, identifying major and minor topics of study, aligning grade-level standards and assessments, identifying mastered and nonmastered content, and providing instruction that emphasizes formal mathematics language, estimates results, analyzes problem outcomes, detects problem fallacies, and utilizes real-life examples

- **Effective instructional delivery** includes interactive teaching, large-and small-group instruction, equity of participation, questioning and facilitating in the classroom, analyzing data to set instructional directions and evaluate mastery, problem-solving strategies, peer teaming, and integrated technology

- **Support resources** include mentoring and tutoring opportunities; a resource bank of reinforcement activities for use by faculty, students, and parents; technology supports; summer and holiday learning packets and/or programs; student business internships; and faculty externships.

A highly effective mathematics classroom is an interactive model in which administrators, teachers, students, parents, and community members all have an integral part.

The fastest growing part of the high school curriculum during the 1980s and 1990s was in Advanced Placement or other college-level courses; over the same time period, the fastest growing part of the college mathematics curriculum was in remedial or high school–level courses.

—Kati Haycock

More important, it is a classroom in which all mathematics content, whether previously mastered or not, can be learned or reinforced.

In many cases, the large number of content standards identified in each grade-level mathematics curriculum leaves teachers feeling the stress of "so much material, so little time." In many cases, mathematics teachers, particularly those teaching accelerated courses, are very negative toward the suggestion of adding nonmastered content and/or reinforcement activities into the course content. "Compared to the mathematics taught in other countries, the typical mathematics curriculum in the U.S....is more noteworthy for the quantity of topics than the quality of content. The result is a mathematics education that is 'a mile wide and an inch deep.' Our young people are 'taught' more topics than their peers in high-achieving nations, but their disappointing performance shows that in this case, more is clearly less" (Haycock, 2002b, p. 10).

From the onset, activities that identify and reinforce areas of mathematics nonmastery must be identified and planned to coincide with the current mathematics instruction goals. These activities must be seen, in fact, as providing a greater opportunity for more students to successfully complete the current course content. Grade-level teachers or mathematics teachers with the same course should identify common instructional goals, curriculum standards, and assessments. Mathematics faculty collaborating with content teachers may discover new opportunities to reinforce nonmastered mathematics skills, understanding the advantage gained in long-term student academic success. Student work and course outcomes should be set in collaboration with the numeracy team and the department or grade-level team, who can identify multiple opportunities for cross-content reinforcement of mathematics skills.

As you increase the participation of all students in mathematics, teachers are required to differentiate instruction for students with diverse mathematics preparation. The need for instructional skills in this area may leave some teachers feeling inadequately prepared. To gain highly qualified certification or to maintain teacher quality, mathematics teachers may need professional training in building a repertoire that improves their skills in differentiating learning activities, in collaborating and teaming with other teachers, and in identifying project-based, real-life activities that utilize mathematics and technology skills to solve problems. Ongoing professional development with the mathematics faculty, designed to support active student learning, will upgrade and maintain the highly qualified skills of teachers in your mathematics department. Increasing mathematics rigor means:

- Faculty consensus around student work
- Increased opportunities for integrating technology
- High expectations for every student
- Student engagement through peer teaming and tutoring
- Interdisciplinary problem solving and real-world activities.

Focusing on rigorous mathematics content, engaging in project-based activities, planning collaboratively, upgrading professional skills, diversifying teaching, utilizing data to identify instructional objectives, and broadening participation of students in mathematics classes will serve as a strong foundation in improving schoolwide numeracy.

NOTES FROM THE FIELD ...

Estrella Foothills High School

Estrella Foothills High School in Goodyear, AZ, opened its doors to its first group of students in August 2001. After working through the infinite number of details, problems, and issues confronting a new school, principal Leslie Standerfer and the mathematics department faced a new challenge: providing an effective instructional program to ensure that students would be successful on the newly mandated state testing, Arizona's Instrument to Measure Standards (AIMS). After much study, discussion, and collaboration, the mathematics department made the following changes to reach this goal:

Alignment: The mathematics teachers were able to quickly identify the courses that covered the material to be tested. These classes were designated as AIMS preparatory courses and became the first four courses a student typically would take at the school.

Common exercises and exams: With these preparatory courses already aligned to the state assessment, the mathematics department created common final exams also aligned with and formatted to the AIMS mathematics standards.

Support for unsuccessful students: Increased attention, including remedial assistance, is focused on students who have been unsuccessful in their first attempt on the mathematics portion of the AIMS test.

Common planning time: All mathematics teachers are members of a professional learning community where they discuss curriculum, instruction, assessments, and individual student progress toward success on the AIMS exam.

Celebration of success: The mathematics department has created a "Mathematics Hall of Fame," where the name of each student who receives the highest distinction on the AIMS exam is posted.

All of this hard work has paid off handsomely. Each year, for the past three years, Estrella Foothills has surpassed the state in AIMS Mathematics Mean Scaled Scores and in 2006 outpaced the state in the percentage of students earning "passing" or "exceeding" ratings by 9 points.

Chapter 4: Promoting a Rigorous Schoolwide Numeracy Program

Estrella Foothills High School: 10th-Grade Mathematics Proficiency (%)

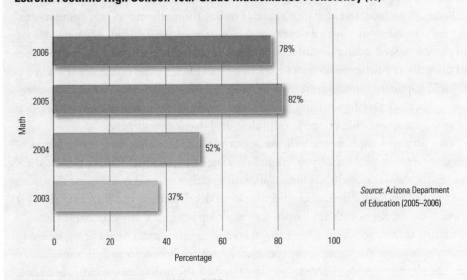

Source: Arizona Department of Education (2005–2006)

The state average for math was 69% in 2006.

Mathematics Instruction in the Rigorous Content Classroom

With all teachers focused on increased academic rigor in every classroom (Chapter 1), the numeracy team must lead them in identifying and discussing *content-area activities and projects* where mathematics and technology are used as problem-solving tools. After identifying grade-level areas of mathematics mastery and nonmastery and reviewing the grade-level mathematics standards, content-area teachers with the support of the numeracy team now plan for areas of instructional overlap. This is the point where mathematics content can be reinforced and mathematics skills can be utilized in instructional activities and projects in all the subject areas. Grade-level and/or departmental staff members need planning time to collaborate and to identify integrated projects with learning tasks that reinforce mathematics skills across the curriculum. Collaborative planning time allows content-area and mathematics teachers to design interdisciplinary opportunities to deepen students' mathematics knowledge and skills. For example, if the mathematics standard, "The student produces evidence that demonstrates understanding of geometry and measurement concepts by solving problems involving scale and by graphing functions in a coordinate system" is a grade-level area of nonmastery, social studies teachers may plan activities that ask students to organize data, read maps, or make graphs, and science teachers may plan activities that ask students to summarize data and predict solution outcomes. Or if the standard is, "The student produces evidence of understanding of number and operation concepts by representing numbers in decimal or fraction form," elective course teachers in culinary arts, music, or physical education may provide instructional support in fractions or decimals by asking students to divide a recipe, look at timing in a musical composition, or calculate player statistics in the sports page. This can be accomplished with the instructional support of the grade-level mathematics teacher providing instruction in statistics or graphing in class. All content-area teachers with the support of the numeracy team or departmental teams should plan activities that ask students to organize information and utilize mathematics as a tool to solve content-area problems.

The good news is that many mathematics organizations, test-preparation companies, district offices, and universities have interactive, interdisciplinary, real-life mathematics projects and activities available online for mathematics and content-area teachers. These low- or no-cost educational resources are available for teachers, tutors, and parents as well. Many interdisciplinary projects might be identified through review and discussion of these resources and might be identified by the numeracy team or an interdisciplinary subcommittee. Identifying real-life activities and projects that use mathematics as a problem-solving tool is clearly more relevant and engaging to students and may be a schoolwide planning or professional development need.

As a principal implementing the recommendations from *Breaking Ranks II* and *Breaking Ranks in the Middle*, you might investigate the potential for flexible scheduling that can provide increased time for collaborative teacher planning, increased classroom time for student instruction, aligned professional development, and increased time for intervention strategies with students whose skills lag behind. Daily classroom visits ensure that comprehensive teaching strategies and rigorous content are being utilized in every classroom. An effective instructional leader, while not necessarily a mathematician, can identify rigorous content standards that clearly utilize mathematics as a tool, differentiation of instruction that draws on prior learning, and social and academic

NOTES FROM THE FIELD …

Georgia O'Keeffe Middle School

Several years ago, Georgia O'Keeffe Middle School in Madison, WI, was faced with declining mathematics scores and needed to take a fresh look at strategies to close the achievement gap and to improve mathematics achievement for every student. As a result of their initial efforts, the middle school was chosen as a 2004 Wisconsin Promise School of Recognition, a school that met Adequate Yearly Progress two or more consecutive years with high percentages of Title I–eligible students. According to former principal Patrick Delmore:

> Giving all students access to a higher quality, more-demanding curriculum was the contributing factor to our success. First, the school made all mathematics classes heterogeneously grouped and reflecting the demographics of our school. Our "exceptional educational needs" and English language learner teachers are integrated into teaching teams and classrooms where they support all students with their learning teams. In mathematics classrooms where students have a variety of experiences and mathematics preparation, teachers differentiate the curriculum, utilize a variety of instructional strategies, and rely on the instructional support of the teachers on the team. Professional development for all teachers was focused on building the teaching skills needed to support powerful mathematics instruction in all content areas.

Principal Kay Enright continued on the course established by her predecessor. Additionally, new resources were obtained to support specific, focused staff development on particular units of study with attention to current areas of student confusion in mathematics. The school developed significant partnerships with the Madison community. Community agencies provided struggling students with a cadre of well-trained, committed tutors and mentors. According to Enright, "The benefit is confident and capable math students who enjoy learning math and teaching each other. Evidence of this is our steadily improving WKCE scores and the numbers of students achieving at high levels on every kind of assessment. The achievement gap is narrowing and our mathematics state scores are the highest they have ever been."

District: Madison Metropolitan School District
O'Keeffe Middle School

Tested Grade(s): 6, 7, 8
Enrollment: 354

Objective	2003–2004		2004–2005		2005–2006	
	AYP	Status	AYP	Status	AYP	Status
I. Test Participation	Yes	Satisfactory	Yes	Satisfactory	Yes	Satisfactory
II. Other Academic Indicator	Yes	Satisfactory	Yes	Satisfactory	Yes	Satisfactory
III. Reading	Yes	Satisfactory	Yes	Satisfactory	Yes	Satisfactory
IV. Mathematics	Yes	Satisfactory	Yes	Satisfactory	Yes	Satisfactory
Met Adequate Yearly Progress?	Yes		Yes		Yes	
Improvement Status:	Satisfactory		Satisfactory		Satisfactory	
					Not Title I	

Key:

Met Adequate Yearly Progress:

Summarizes the overall attainment of the AYP objectives. Beginning with 2002–2003, all four objectives must be met (indicated above by a "Yes" or an "Improved" level for each objective—I. Test Participation, II. Other Academic Indicator, III. Reading, and IV. Mathematics). A "No" indicates that AYP was not met. AYP must be missed in the same objective for two consecutive years for Improvement Status to begin.

equity for all students in the classroom. Through initiating interactive professional development activities such as those described in Chapter 1, content-area teachers may begin to identify anticipated teacher and student behaviors in the "rigorous mathematics classroom." The opportunities to improve mathematics mastery in a schoolwide interdisciplinary initiative will certainly go a long way toward improving student mathematics skills and closing the numeracy gap.

The Role of Technology in the Rigorous Classroom

Welcome to the 21st century—and a continuation of the Calculator Wars! Some educators embrace technology to augment the academic preparation of students planning to attend university and other postsecondary programs where incoming students are required to purchase a computer for their studies. These educators also perceive technological literacy as crucial to success in the workplace.

Other educators witness the perils that await students online, fear the reduced fundamental-skills practice time, and mistrust project completion from unidentified Internet sources. These educators are concerned that the convenience of technology may hinder students in the acquisition of fundamental mathematics skill development, in estimating logical solutions, and in determining fallacies in evidence. If the calculator provides students an answer—any answer—students often don't stop to deliberate if the answer is reasonable, teachers lament.

Illustration by Mark Jordan

Yet, as the war continues, so does the proliferation of technology in schools. Schools introduce handheld calculators in high school science and mathematics classes, fund "hubbed" interactive technology in classes so teachers can evaluate a range of responses and discuss problem solutions in real time, and even provide a laptop to every student in the school. There has been overt support of the introduction of calculators in elementary and middle school mathematics classes and the use of computers at every grade level for writing, researching, and problem solving. The move to technology in secondary schools precedes any definitive research to support its use. Yet the use of technology is commonplace to accelerate instruction in all content areas or reinforce instruction in others—or for benchmark testing and receiving immediate and detailed error diagnostics of the results. For every step forward, however, there are many steps backward, and the tug-of-war over evaluating the success of technology continues while the use of technology in the classroom, effective or ineffective, grows.

Technology growth has impacted the staff and administration. Many districts not only have assigned every teacher a laptop computer but also have assigned every administrator and other staff-supervisors both a computer and a personal digital assistant (PDA). The computers support teachers in classroom management areas such as assignment preparation, parent communication, substitute allocations, attendance, testing, grading, and collaboration with other teachers. The PDA has been adopted in an effort to help administrators and supervisors become more effective by enhancing organization and improving communication with district offices. Technology supports administrators and supervisors in facilities maintenance, accountability management, and communication with all education stakeholders.

In the classroom, technology is a tool that, when properly implemented, should move mathematics mastery forward. However, all technology should be introduced with a robust professional development program so that staff will begin to see usage results commensurate with the cost of the equipment.

Chapter 4: Promoting a Rigorous Schoolwide Numeracy Program

Increasing Mathematics Rigor

The staff at Lake Highlands Junior High School in Richardson, TX, experienced annual concern regarding declining student passing rates on state assessment testing (TAKS). Socioeconomic pressures and a variety of other special circumstances make it difficult for many students to perform to their potential in mathematics and in math-related subjects. However, thanks to a joint mathematics intervention technology initiative, average student results on the TAKS have turned around at Lake Highlands. This unusual program involved increased mathematics rigor supported by new technology to assist students in communicating their mathematical thinking and to provide immediate feedback regarding their mathematical knowledge. According to Principal Lorine Burrell, "The test results prove that when you provide care, time, and technology and have high expectations, the students are going to rise to the occasion." Based on the success of the pilot, the program was expanded in Richardson for the 2006–07 school year.

Mathematics Program

_____ Ensure a rigorous mathematics program by:

    _____ Analyzing schoolwide mathematics data to complete school and individual profiles

    _____ Engaging faculty in discussions about building consensus for evaluating student work

    _____ Developing interdisciplinary high-performing, collaborative teacher teams

    _____ Utilizing stakeholders and data to develop a Numeracy Improvement Plan

    _____ Providing opportunities for teacher growth

    _____ Engaging parents and community

    _____ Committing resources for mathematics improvement

    _____ Providing support programs for students and parents

    _____ Monitoring good classroom instruction

    _____ Scheduling planning opportunities for teachers

    _____ Raising expectation levels

    _____ Encouraging student enrollment in mathematics each year

    _____ Identifying and providing summer learning opportunities in mathematics for teachers and students.

Content Classroom

_____ Support mathematics instruction in the content classroom by:

    _____ Assisting content teachers with identifying areas of instructional overlap

    _____ Assisting content teachers with planning activities that require students to organize content information and utilize mathematics as a tool to solve problems

    _____ Adopting flexible scheduling techniques

    _____ Making daily classroom visits

    _____ Providing professional development to help content teachers identify and practice rigorous classroom instruction behaviors.

Technology

_____ Ensure that technology is properly integrated schoolwide by:

    _____ Monitoring its effect as a tool toward moving mathematics mastery forward

    _____ Integrating technology fundamentals into a strong professional development program

    _____ Taking steps to provide adequate funding on an ongoing basis.

5 Hiring and Developing Teachers as Partners in Numeracy

School Improvement is actually a very simple concept…
- *Get better teachers*
- *Improve the teachers you have.*

—*Todd Whitaker*

"One of the strongest predictors of student success is the quality of their teachers" (Capital Area Institute for Mathematics and Science, Penn State, n.d., p. 1). It seems obvious that without excellent teachers, schools will never reach the goal of high achievement for all students. In implementing a whole-school numeracy initiative, principals quickly recognize the key to increased student achievement does, indeed, lie in ensuring that the school has effective, well-trained, and motivated mathematics and other content-area teachers. In addition, the entire school community must be committed to providing a curriculum that meets high standards, using differentiated instructional strategies, and supporting students to ensure that they leave high school having mastered the necessary competencies. In all such schoolwide improvement initiatives, the recruiting, hiring, retaining, and ongoing development of highly qualified classroom teachers is central to the success of the students.

School Interview Team

To ensure that the school hires new staff members who support the school's philosophy and initiatives, the principal's responsibility is to designate an interview team who will structure the interview questions, score the responses, and serve as representatives of the school and community in the interview, screening and identifying new teachers. The team must evaluate responses to carefully fashioned interview questions that are designed to determine whether or not the candidate shares the vision in the school improvement and numeracy improvement plans that express high expectations for all students and is committed to meeting mastery targets through teacher-diversified instruction. The interview team includes representatives from:

- Administrative/leadership teams
- Numeracy team
- Department/grade-level teams
- Teachers from the content area (may serve as designated)
- Community or parent leader representative
- Student leader representative.

Prior to the interview, the team needs to thoroughly discuss school demographic data to identify performance factors needed to successfully staff the school. This dynamic profile may help to recruit and carefully select qualified teachers for the numeracy initiative. Data may help the team find a "twofer"—perhaps a content teacher who may be able to analyze data or utilize technology particularly well; a teacher who may be willing to tutor before, during, or after the school day; a teacher who may have dual content certification; or a bilingual teacher who is certified in a content area. A teacher who is willing and capable of taking on more than one role within the school is invaluable at any time, but is especially helpful when launching a new initiative.

In the hiring process, the interview team should formulate questions and listen for evidence of proficiency in three areas:

Knowledge	Skills	Attitudes/Beliefs

Content major
Content minor
Reading classes
Mathematics classes
Technology classes
	Practice opportunities such as:
	  Tutoring
	  Supervised teaching
	  Coaching
	  Mentoring
	  Volunteering
		Vision includes all students
		High expectations
		Teaming
		Flexibility
		Interdisciplinary curriculum

Documentation		

Transcripts:
  Undergrad
  Grad
  Continuing education
    courses
  Technology classes
Certificates
Responses to interview
  questions
	Résumé
	Responses to interview
	  questions
	References
	Videotapes of classroom
	  performance
		Responses to interview
		  questions
		References

One School's Hiring Plan

According to Georgia O'Keeffe Middle School (Madison, WI) former Principal Patrick Delmore:

"When teaching openings occur at our school, we post a detailed job description that outlines the expectations, skills, and training that candidates need. An interview team that includes me, school math teachers, and local school support staff members conducts interviews for potential teacher transfers from other districts or hires from outside the district. This process helps us find skilled staff members who buy into our beliefs, curriculum, and pedagogy."

(2005, p. 42)

Professional Development for Numeracy

Implementing a whole-school numeracy action plan is vastly different, in many respects, from other secondary whole-school reform efforts. Often, in their teacher training or continuing education programs, teachers have not had sufficient preparation in the basic foundations of a solid numeracy initiative, such as differentiating learning activities, collaborating with other teachers, developing project-based activities that utilize mathematics as a problem-solving tool, or utilizing data to direct instruction. In addition, identifying real-life–based projects and problem-solving techniques that utilize the community as a classroom may also likely surface as a critical professional development topic. Although technology is present in many school environments, opportunities to integrate it into the classroom as a simulation tool or to utilize it as an instructional tool may be limited by teacher preparation or resources, or both. This may provide an additional area for collaborative, ongoing professional development and planning. It is often assumed that most secondary teachers are relatively strong in content knowledge, but many teachers actually have major needs in this area. Some issues may arise from the assignment of classes in the teacher's weakest area or may happen due to curriculum changes resulting in the introduction of courses teachers may not have taken in college, such as probability and statistics or discrete mathematics for mathematics teachers or journalism or technical writing for English teachers. This lack of preparation of teachers in their content areas, particularly mathematics, complicates the implementation of the Numeracy Improvement Plan and must be addressed in a comprehensive professional development plan.

As you and your numeracy team begin to evaluate faculty needs and monitor staff development, remember that powerful staff development should be the focus of every faculty meeting, team meeting, peer observation, discussion about student work, and planning time. Use the discussion around the components in Figure 5-1 for formulating and evaluating the plan.

FIGURE 5-1
Powerful Staff Development: Planning for Knowing and Growing

COMPONENT	KEY QUESTIONS
Identifying Faculty Needs For Staff Development	What staff development needs were identified as priorities by the staff? What knowledge and skills identified in the School Numeracy Profile need to be studied? What teacher skills in differentiating instruction need to be studied? Has your staff discussed the numeracy plan and identified potential areas for instructional growth? Which identified topics need large- or small-group instruction/workshops? Do methods to integrate technology into content classes need to be studied? Can all staff effectively utilize assessment data to inform instruction? What skills and knowledge need to be studied to make the improvement plan a reality?

OUTCOMES

Strategies to support the mathematics weaknesses identified in the School Numeracy Profile and effective teaching of students with diverse mathematics preparation relies heavily on a repertoire of instructional strategies. If the faculty is to build the capacity for successful plan implementation, the numeracy team must address and support a professional development plan that provides knowledge and skill acquisition in the following areas:

- Content/subject matter
- Classroom management
- Teaching practices
- Instruction, driven by assessment
- Technology integration
- Differentiated instruction
- Group dynamics/collaborative teams
- Teachers as instructional leaders
- Cross-curriculum strategies
- Authentic evaluation of student work
- Authentic evaluation of student work
- Mathematics in the content area.

After each staff meeting/discussion, use the key questions in Figure 5-2, and others tailored to your school and situation, as the framework for evaluation of the effectiveness of the activities and the overall plan.

FIGURE 5-2

Monitoring the Staff Development Plan

COMPONENT	KEY QUESTIONS
Monitoring and Evaluating Staff Development	Is training content relative to my current teaching assignment?
	Is staff applying the strategies and content to enrich students' experiences?
	What was the most effective staff development activity that I have completed?
	Have teachers gained the knowledge to develop cross-curricular instructional materials that utilize mathematics skills as a tool?
	Have teachers utilized data to diversify classroom instruction?
	Have teachers developed real-life activities and interdisciplinary projects that utilize problem-solving skills, mathematics skills, and technology tools?
	Have teachers aligned instruction to nonmastered curriculum standards?

OUTCOMES
Powerful staff development means planning for knowing and growing. A professional development plan is only effective if information is utilized to impact student achievement. Monitoring the implementation of what has been presented and what was effective and useful in the classroom with students is the standard by which to judge the effectiveness of your plan.
Effective staff development focuses every meeting, every team planning session, every peer observation, and every learning expectation on students and student work.

Chapter 5: Hiring and Developing Teachers as Partners in Numeracy

Because the numeracy professional development challenge is twofold, the school community needs to build capacity in the school staff in several ways: giving content-area teachers support in developing and teaching content-specific instructional activities utilizing mathematics as a problem-solving tool and giving mathematics teachers instructional support in teaching interactive mathematics courses and developing interdisciplinary activities that support mathematics skills in problem solving.

The Logic Model of Professional Development simply and effectively demonstrates the central role that a quality professional development program plays. As their knowledge and skills develop, coupled with their improved classroom instruction through practice, classroom teachers and their supervising teachers and administrators will see much-improved student performance.

Logic Model of Professional Development

Quality of PD program
↓
Increased Teacher Knowledge/Skills
↓
Improved Classroom Practice
↓
Improved Student Performance

Iris R. Weiss (2006, p. 10)

Some groups, such as the National Staff Development Council (NSDC), are most interested in the process of staff development, regardless of content, with the expressed outcome remaining the same. According to NSDC, "The primary purpose of staff development is to ensure high levels of learning for all students through improved professional development learning experiences for every school employee who affects student learning" (Sparks, 2001, p. 1).

Effective professional development means building a culture of ongoing learning for the adults in a school as well as the students.

—Loucks-Horsely, Stiles, and Hewson (1996, p. 5)

Developing mathematics teachers

Unfortunately, very few of our most experienced mathematics or other content teachers have been trained to lead change and build collaborative learning communities. To build momentum for transformation within their departments, the most accomplished mathematics teachers need assistance, via professional development opportunities, in acquiring or perfecting leadership skills to support school change utilizing collaboration, team building, and consensus. New or very inexperienced mathematics teachers come with a different set of issues not easily resolved. They are often overwhelmed and discouraged in a short period of time. "One third of America's new teachers leave sometime during their first three years, and almost half depart after the first five years" (Fulton, Burns, and Goldenberg, 2005, p. 299). In a recent study, Sterling (2004) noted that for mathematics teachers, the turnover rate is even higher than for teachers in general.

Inexperienced teachers often have a limited repertoire of knowledge and skills and, unfortunately, little support is provided by textbooks. In a detailed review of mathematics and science textbooks, the American Association for the Advancement of Science found "mathematics textbooks particularly lacking in effective instructional strategies" (Haycock, 2002b, p. 11), a critical area for new mathematics teachers. This problem is compounded when experienced teachers teach accelerated course offerings, leaving less-experienced teachers with the responsibility of working with more challenging students who have a broader range of mathematics skill preparation. All staff development need not be addressed in a large group but designed and tailored around the needs of a subset of teachers. New or inexperienced teachers may need professional development in classroom management and instructional techniques while some experienced staff members may benefit from mentor or coaches training.

In an attempt to discover whether representatives of the mathematics (and science) communities share a common understanding of what defines effective professional learning experiences and how teacher development should be supported, the Professional Development Project of the National Institute for Science Educators examined a variety of standards and related materials, including items developed by the National Council of Teachers of Mathematics (NCTM), the National Center for Improving Science Education, the U.S. Department of Education, and independent researchers. A common "vision" was reached, encompassing seven "best practices principles" for professional development in both mathematics and science.

Professional development experiences should be:

1. Driven by a clear, well-defined image of effective classroom learning and teaching

2. Provide teachers with opportunities to develop knowledge and skills and broaden their teaching approaches, so that they can create better learning opportunities for students

3. Use instructional methods to promote learning for adults that mirror the methods to be used with students

4. Build or strengthen the learning community of science and mathematics teachers

5. Prepare and support teachers to serve in leadership roles if they are inclined to do so

6. Provide links to other parts of the educational system

7. Include continuous assessment.

Loucks-Horsley et al. (1996)

NCTM parallels the Logic Model of Professional Development by emphasizing staff development activities that focus on improving knowledge and understanding of the subject matter (*increased teacher knowledge/skills*), teaching methods (*improved classroom practice*), and assessment (*improved student performance*). According to NCTM, "The professional development of teachers of mathematics is a process of learning: learning mathematics and about mathematics; learning about students and how they learn, individually and in the social setting of school;…learning the craft of teaching… learning new ways to develop mathematical power in all students" (National Council of Teachers of Mathematics, n.d.).

Professional Development That Supports Numeracy

The current needs of the school staff can be identified through observation, needs assessments/surveys (see Appendix 8), and formal and informal discussions. Not only are the needs of each teacher subgroup (e.g., experienced vs. inexperienced, mathematics vs. other content areas) different, but each faculty member's independent concerns and worries may not fit nicely into the current vision that you, as the school leader or the leadership team member, may have. Thus it is extremely important that the purposes of the professional development are identified and agreed upon early in the process. Although the overarching goal may be to provide the background experiences and training necessary to successfully implement a numeracy initiative, the teachers involved will have multiple learning needs to reach that goal. The different purposes of your professional development must address those needs and may include strengthening content knowledge, understanding how students learn, learning how to select rigorous career-oriented instructional materials, acquiring new instructional strategies, and/or gaining information about curriculum alignment and assessment practices. It is crucial that professional development designers take into account the teachers' current level of knowledge in each of these areas.

In addition, the principal must have the foresight to anticipate the obstructions that may be encountered in designing an effective professional development program. Barriers such as teacher attitudes from previous poorly designed professional development experiences, union pressures, limited school system support, lack of resources, or community apathy all can impede the progress of any initiative. When these issues are being addressed, decisions must be made about professional development strategies and materials. Principals must think beyond the traditional workshop model to other types of innovative delivery systems that go further than simply presenting information to teachers. If teachers are being asked to "connect the dots" between careers and content for students, professional development activities for teachers should model the same principles for them. Business and industry partners may provide real-life experiences or training curricula that transfer effectively to the classroom. Partnerships with scientists and mathematicians at the university or in business or industry should be encouraged. Teacher externships during the year or in the summer certainly would give teachers a more realistic view of the importance of numeracy skills in the workplace. These workplace experiences could be structured to introduce practices that integrate numeracy experiences, immerse teachers in problem-solving and inquiry activities, and utilize the actual content and curriculum required in their classrooms. It is wise to investigate a wide variety of strategies such as inquiry-immersion workshops, action research, case study discussions, and examination of student work.

The principal plays a crucial role in ensuring that this vision of effective professional development is successful. The principal must first be confident in his or her ability to lead this change and must seek district-level, state, or outside assistance to supplement areas of weakness or concern. Targeted professional development for educational leaders to effectively change school culture is as important as the training designed to enhance teaching and learning skills of teachers. For those leaders who seek assistance in identifying and focusing on a professional development plan, NASSP offers an online assessment tool that enables administrators to identify leadership strengths and weaknesses and devise an individual development plan for growth (www.principals.org/skillsassessment).

How others perceive your strengths and weaknesses is also beneficial in this assessment process, so the online assessment tool includes a 360-degree assessment to compare how you see yourself with how others see you. Staff must also be encouraged to embrace new and additional roles, such as team leader, department chair, curriculum developer, instructional specialist, staff development facilitator, and assessment specialist and must be willing to be active participants in major initiatives and projects.

At the school level, the principal is charged with creating time within the schedule for professional development activities. Teachers need regularly scheduled blocks of time to work together away from students and other duties and responsibilities. The principal and the leadership team must creatively examine not only the schedule, but staff assignments and time allocations. The overall school structure must be modified to support a collaborative learning environment for teachers.

It is essential that you find ways to provide time and support for collaborative efforts among teams, departments, grade levels, and others responsible for curriculum and content issues with the staff members responsible for planning professional development activities. Often, these are two separate areas of responsibility, with different funding streams, so you must find ways to link the two. Encouraging each group to accept membership on your leadership team provides an excellent vehicle to ensure time together for collaboration and ongoing communication.

The school leader must model the same behaviors expected of the teachers and other staff members: stay flexible, keep communication open, encourage innovation, value mathematics-supported teaching and learning activities in the classroom, and monitor the impact of the changes. Maintain the focus on students and student achievement and, in every meeting or planning session, discuss student work, share best practices, discuss instructional strategies, and identify student learning styles. Each of these items contributes to an effective learning environment from the classroom to the main office.

Finally, the principal accepts responsibility for implementing a strong evaluation component for all professional development efforts. When developing the evaluation, be sure both short- and long-term impacts on the teachers and students are thoroughly examined. The principal and the administrative/leadership team must return to the overarching goal of the numeracy initiative, review the purposes of the staff development program, and assess the success of the program toward building capacity to reach the numeracy goal.

Hiring Teachers

_____ Designate an interview team with a wide range of representatives from the school community to make recommendations for hiring

_____ Formulate substantive questions for the candidates and a method of evaluating responses

_____ Require substantial documentation from candidates in three areas of performance: knowledge, skill, and attitudes/beliefs.

Professional Development (PD)

_____ Develop a plan for schoolwide professional development which includes:

  _____ Identifying current faculty needs for staff development?

  _____ Monitoring the staff development plan on an ongoing basis

  _____ Evaluating the staff development plan

  _____ Utilizing each faculty meeting, team meeting, and other times to focus on staff development

  _____ Ensuring that PD experiences are based on "best practices principles" for mathematics and science

  _____ Anticipating barriers and obstructions to the program

  _____ Presenting experiences that go beyond the "workshop" model

  _____ Requesting real-life experiences for teachers from business and industry partners

_____ Assist new content teachers by:

  _____ Encouraging reflection on classroom best practices

  _____ Providing mentoring and modeling support and experiences

  _____ Providing support for management issues, such as time, organization, planning, resources, and materials

  _____ Providing expert assistance with curriculum and instruction issues

_____ Develop mathematics teachers by:

  _____ Helping leaders acquire skills to support school change

  _____ Taking care when assigning teachers' classes to take strengths, weaknesses, background, and experience into account

  _____ Providing content professional development to bolster weak areas.

Role of the Principal

_____ Evaluate objectively your ability to lead change

_____ Seek assistance to supplement your areas of weakness

_____ Create time within the schedule for PD activities for the staff

_____ Modify the school structure to ensure a collaborative learning environment for teachers

_____ Encourage staff to take on new and/or additional roles

_____ Bring together the teachers and the PD providers for maximum effectiveness

_____ Model the behaviors desired of your staff, such as flexibility, open communication and innovation

_____ Accept responsibility for implementing a strong evaluation component for all PD efforts.

Chapter 5: Hiring and Developing Teachers as Partners in Numeracy

6 Budgeting and Stakeholder Support

Education improves an individual's and community's standard of living.... [P]rincipals are in a unique position to influence their community to fully support state and local school budgets.

—Bill Owings and Leslie Kaplan

As you work through the details of this numeracy initiative, you will find that increased funding may be necessary for effective, continuous implementation. You may also need additional funding for professional development, teacher released time for collaborative planning, additional staff to support instruction, new or additional technology and software in the classroom, and supplemental classroom and reinforcement materials.

Building a Budget

Each year, principals face numerous budget challenges. After adjusting the budget to deal with fixed costs and overhead, principals may feel they lack sufficient funds to finance all the other genuine implementation needs at the school, including requests from excellent staff members or departments needing "extras" to improve instruction. Many times, the support for implementation of new programs or initiatives is far down the list of funding priorities. As you struggle to fund individual requests and well-intentioned school initiatives and programs, your stakeholders' eyes are on you because they believe you will fund first what's most important to you.

Ideally, the budget process should take place in an environment that is open to input from the entire school but maintains a goal-oriented focus. You must be certain that the school dedicates sufficient funding to meet its personnel requirements and other annual obligations first. Then the school must act on the most pressing curricular and instructional needs—such as the Numeracy Improvement Plan—and still have a contingency fund or reserves for emergencies, unforeseen occurrences, or cost overruns. It is important that the school leadership and each department/grade-level team make budget requests based on the improvements specifically identified in the Numeracy Improvement Plan.

Building a fiscally responsible budget entails educating the staff and school community about how to interpret a school budget and how it is developed each year. A short lesson on how your building allocation is determined will answer many questions and assist in providing a deeper understanding of this process. Focus on how the building allocation from the district office is determined and disbursed. Working from these figures, spell out the limitations around expending funds in certain categories, such as fixed administrative expenses, personnel, federal and state earmarked funds, etc. After working through all of the required expenditures and setting aside a predetermined percentage for emergencies, the remaining funds should be available for discretionary use by the school, subject to any limits imposed by the district or state. It is important to understand that, in the final analysis, each school has a modest amount—often as little as 5%—of the total budget to utilize for this purpose. At this point, it is wise to introduce the concept of "trimming" some areas of the school budget to support funding for additional professional development, substitutes, hardware and software, or other priorities identified in the improvement plan. Particular care must be taken to work closely with the administrative and teacher leaders to ensure that they receive a sound foundation in this area because they will be instrumental in providing guidance to others. They will help make choices about funding in the areas of curriculum and instruction as well as provide input into decisions about other schoolwide issues.

To align the budget with the goals of the Numeracy Improvement Plan, the principal and the numeracy team should lead the staff in an exercise in which clearly defined school numeracy goals are set for the upcoming year (see Chapter 1). As an integral part of this process, the mathematics and numeracy instructional needs of the school must be prioritized. The outcome should be to recommend sufficient funding to add mathematics courses and electives, upgrade the rigor in the existing mathematics program, implement mathematics across all content areas, provide resources for planning and purchasing supplemental equipment, and determine other expenses to be incurred in schoolwide implementation. For the principal to discuss these requests in detail with the stakeholders, a numeracy program budget worksheet should be devised, which, when completed, makes the explicit connection between the schoolwide numeracy goals and spending requests. (See Appendix 9 for a sample template.) Departments and/or grade-level teams should be given a quick inservice lesson on how best to work collaboratively to complete this form. It should then be returned to the principal to be examined in conjunction with all of the other department or team requests. The principal, after collating and synthesizing the requests into one schoolwide document, should devise a feedback mechanism whereby all of the staff has an opportunity to provide input into the final decisions regarding what to fund. This can be done in a variety of ways: small-group interdisciplinary discussions, department or team discussions, faculty meetings, or in writing. Gathering this information with input from everyone concerned will help give clarity and equity to the final decision-making process.

Finding Additional Resources

In addition to closely scrutinizing the school budget allocation to utilize all funds to the utmost advantage, you must look to the district for additional resources, especially for expensive items such as ongoing staff development or schoolwide technology. Also, there may be opportunities on the district level for pilot programs that may bring resources to the numeracy initiative to provide professional development, computer hardware and software with companion activities, additional classroom technology, or curriculum resources.

Many private sector science and/or mathematics foundations provide funding for mathematics improvement initiatives. In addition, many schools qualify for additional funding for mathematics and science under federal programs that provide monies from proposal and grant opportunities. The Mathematics and Science Partnership Program (Title II, Part B), which was established to increase the academic achievement of students in mathematics (and science) by enhancing the content knowledge and teaching skills of classroom teachers, is one such example. Detailed information can be found at www.ed.gov/policy/elsec/leg/esea02/pg26.html. There are numerous funding opportunities sponsored by the Mathematical and Physical Science (MPS) program (www.nsf.gov/dir/index.jsp?org=MPS), an arm of the National Science Foundation. Under Title I, money is set aside for the establishment of mathematics and science education partnerships to improve secondary instruction in those areas.

Having involved community stakeholders at the onset may be an advantage in securing additional resources for schoolwide mathematics improvement. An often overlooked resource is found in developing and maintaining effective community partnerships. As defined in the *How-To Guide for School-Business Partnerships*, a partnership is "a mutually supportive relationship between a business and a school or school district in which the partners commit to specific goals and activities intended to benefit students and schools" (Council for Corporate & School Partnerships, n.d., p. 2). This guide lists a wide variety of activities that have been undertaken through partnerships: professional, curricular/instructional, and policy development; guidance, mentoring, and tutoring; incentives and awards; and material and financial resources. Many businesses and organizations are willing to donate instructional support items such as computer hardware and software, expendable supplies for classrooms and labs, library collections, or other supplies and materials. An in-kind partnership program with a local newspaper may provide newspapers and other benefits to the school. These resources can provide opportunities for activities that are interdisciplinary, collaborative, and aligned to real-life experiences that support the Numeracy Improvement Plan.

Examples of donations that could be used as teacher or student incentives or rewards are movie passes, tickets to local sporting events, public transportation passes and tokens, or retail coupons and gift certificates. Do not fail to explore the use of company or corporate volunteers, which may be utilized in a wide variety of ways, when examining this alternative. The Comprehensive Checklist for Partnering and additional planning and assessment templates also can be found in the *How-To Guide for School-Business Partnerships* on www.principals.org.

In addition to formal school–business partnerships, many local employers are eager to improve the quantitative skills of their future workforce and are a source of real-life curriculum and testing materials, hardware and software, and program volunteers. Many government agencies are encouraged by management to form partnerships with local schools to benefit students and improve their educational experiences. The principal and other team members may develop collaborative relationships with not only the business community and government agencies but also the university community. These academic partnerships may increase the material and human resources necessary for numeracy program implementation and provide rich opportunities for professional development. Finally, it is well known that parent groups, if properly motivated, also provide extensive program resources through fundraising efforts, workplace networks, and volunteerism. Parent and community activists who are aware of the goals of the school can serve as liaisons to identify and form partnership alliances. The principal, with the assistance of others, must be focused in identifying resources and adopting programs that provide for the schools' identified priority needs and, in particular, those in support of the initiatives of the schoolwide Numeracy Improvement Plan.

NOTES FROM THE FIELD …

Lake Highlands Junior High School

Lake Highlands Junior High School in Richardson, TX, is just one of hundreds of schools across the country whose students have benefited from a business partnership. In 2005, the Richardson Independent School District entered into a joint mathematics intervention initiative with the district and Texas Instruments (TI) and designated Lake Highlands as a model pilot school for the 2005–06 school year. After significant professional development, the teachers improved and enriched classroom instruction and assessment and enhanced students' mathematical understanding through the use of TI advanced graphing calculators and the TI-Navigator system, which provides wireless communication between the students' TI graphing calculators and the teacher's PC to provide in-classroom networks. In what has become known as the "Richardson Model," the students participated in daily lessons in which they were required to solve problems, communicate solutions, apply content, and connect mathematical models to abstract concepts. The technology allowed the teachers to monitor each student's progress on a screen as concepts were taught and problems worked, allowing for immediate feedback and opportunities for intervention. As a result of the intervention made possible by this partnership, 33% of the students who had previously failed the state test in 2005 successfully passed in 2006. Individual test scores increased by an average of six points, and the program's students showed continual improvement on benchmark assessment exams given throughout the year. Lake Highlands made AYP under NCLB, and the district moved from "acceptable" to "recognized" under the Texas accountability rating system.

_____ Educate the staff about how a budget is built each year

_____ Educate the staff about how to interpret the local school budget document

_____ Align the relevant components of the budget with the Numeracy Improvement Plan

_____ Determine the amount of money available to fund the numeracy initiative

_____ Create a budget worksheet for use by individuals, teams, and departments

_____ Summarize the results and solicited discussion from school leaders and the full staff

_____ Prioritize the numeracy initiative proposed expenditures

_____ Use the district as a resource for items not funded under the local school budget

_____ Explore federal grants and other sources outside the district for funding

_____ Utilize the _How-To Guide for School-Business Partnerships_ as a resource to develop and maintain effective school–business partnerships

_____ Look to local colleges and universities for assistance

_____ Solicit assistance from parent groups.

7 Monitoring and Evaluating

What gets monitored gets done.

The principal performs two critically important tasks that will ultimately determine the success of the Numeracy Improvement Plan. One undertaking is to establish an effective numeracy team (see Chapter 2) whose goal is to design and implement the school's numeracy program, coordinating with teachers who are implementing the program in their individual classes and establishing a process for student engagement. This group will ultimately make or break the numeracy initiative.

The principal's second important task is to continue to directly observe the implementation of the program in the classroom. Following up on a regular basis shows that the principal is serious about expecting change. The school leaders (including members of the numeracy team), following the example set by the principal, must be in classrooms on a daily basis, observing, coaching, and supporting staff members while encouraging students to master concepts taught in their mathematics classes and to apply their numeracy skills and knowledge to solve problems in their content classes.

The manner in which education decisions are made takes many forms—some through trial and error in the classroom, others through more formal processes. With guidance and input, the numeracy team will make many curricular and instructional decisions prior to the numeracy plan's implementation by classroom teachers. To better understand what needs to be accomplished, every member of the team leading the numeracy improvement efforts needs to be in classrooms—observing and coaching—every day. A large part of the principal's job is to facilitate the decision-making process and then, with team members, monitor the results of those decisions.

Methods must be devised to track the progress of students, analyze the results of different teaching methods, and discern the value of various materials used. The results of these monitoring activities allow the principal to evaluate the effectiveness of both the individual class and whole-school programs and make necessary adjustments and improvements over time, especially in designing effective, ongoing professional development and identifying best-practice classroom activities. Careful and continuous monitoring is an integral part of an effective numeracy program because it gives feedback to the numeracy team to help classroom teachers determine the most effective strategies for teaching numeracy and because it helps teachers address students' individual learning problems that may seriously interfere with their achievement.

Monitoring a school numeracy program is a systematic process of examining the curriculum and resources, teachers' instructional strategies, and the resulting student performance in order to improve the mathematics achievement of students. This monitoring process includes three stages:

1. Periodically collect relevant data

2. Analyze and evaluate the information

3. Take action, when necessary, to improve student performance.

Prior to taking these steps, it is important for the principal and numeracy team to be clear on the answers to the questions: *"What are we evaluating and why?"* The answers must be shared and discussed in detail with teachers. When an entire school is able to articulate their numeracy goals for students and the types of evidence they need to determine whether students are successful in meeting those goals, they have built a foundation for the monitoring process as well as for learning.

Simply stated, monitoring a numeracy improvement initiative requires a continuous process of tracking and evaluating procedures and outcomes. Think about faculty consensus regarding desired teacher and student behaviors. (See Appendix 3). Principals must enlist the assistance of content teachers in providing data on students' achievement and success in the numeracy activities in their classrooms. During formal and informal classroom observations, the principal seeks evidence in each and every classroom that the teacher is creating an appropriate learning environment and employing a wide range of teaching strategies matched to students' needs. At the same time, teachers must be held accountable for creating opportunities for numeracy development in a planned way within the curriculum content standards and making appropriate use of instructional technology to enhance learning. Consider developing a classroom observation checklist from these discussions and look for the following evidence:

- Planning
- Curriculum standards
- Classroom management
- Equity of participation
- Differentiated instruction
- Questioning techniques
- Cooperative learning
- Student engagement
- Interdisciplinary instruction
- Problem-solving activities
- Technology integration
- Activities requiring high-level thinking.

Remember, several different types of monitoring can provide data over time:

- **Daily visits** throughout the school year are good for the principal, the teacher, the students, and the school. As the principal increases his or her visibility in the classroom, he or she is able to acquire general impressions over time, and can note other concerns or problems (facilities, attendance, training, equipment, etc.) in addition to observing daily instruction.

- The **walk-through** is similar in some ways to a daily visit, but far more focused. This activity, which is intended to be separate from the formal teacher evaluation process, involves visiting every classroom at a specific time interval (daily, weekly, biweekly) for a short period of time (e.g., 3 to 15 minutes) with a specific objective or question in mind. The procedure varies in each school on the basis of philosophy, need, intent, and other critical factors such as school size. For example, at Arroyo High School, each week every administrator makes five-minute visits to five different classrooms conducting "power walk-throughs" and uses a structured protocol to provide specific feedback to the teachers. School district staff also carries out theme-focused schoolwide observations and provides formal feedback to the principal (Mero et al., 2005). Principals employing this method consistently agree that walk-throughs are a useful means of helping teachers reflect about teaching and learning and engaging the teacher and principal in a dialogue about best practices and progress toward schoolwide goals. As Principal Deepi Kang-Weisz at Edenrose Public School (Ontario, Canada) shares: "When I do classroom walk-throughs, I am looking for best practices determined by a reflective question that focuses on a practice or strategy our staff has determined to be a priority. The process is an informal and nonevaluative one; its purpose is to foster reflective practice" (Hopkins, 2006, p. 2). These types of observations are important because they provide firm data to affirm perceptions. Arroyo has refined this process even further by conducting math walk-throughs developed through a partnership between the mathematics department and the University of California at Los Angeles. A committee of professors and teachers conducts observations to find ways to improve curriculum alignment, mathematics mastery, and instructional strategies (Mero et al., 2005).

- Most school districts require **formal evaluations** of each teacher on a periodic basis. Many supply the specific criteria, strict procedures, timeline, and even the forms to be completed. When incorporating numeracy goals into the formal evaluation, care must be given to integrate these goals with the purposes and procedures required by the district and/or state. One course of action is to not only be sure that during every observation required for the formal evaluation, required procedures are strictly followed but also maximize that opportunity to gather information regarding the successful implementation of the goals of the Numeracy Improvement Plan in the teacher's classroom and discuss this evidence at every conference. To make this task easier, it is suggested that an additional form be created by the school leaders and numeracy team for observers to use during the formal observation process. Once again, refer to the important information gathered from the teachers regarding teaching and learning descriptors (Chapter 1) to formulate a form that is unique to your school's goals and objectives. A sample format to help you get started can be found in Appendix 10.

It is important to remember: "Principals aren't 'encouraged' to be instructional leaders through…simple routines and requirements, they *become* better instructional leaders," according to Mike Schmoker (2001, p. 117). Schmoker goes on to quote a former director of instruction in the Brazosport Independent School District, Patricia Davenport:

> The principal is *required* to go into classrooms, to become a stronger instructional leader by seeing how teachers teach kids. They must be in there…. If two weeks go by, the kids or teachers will come by and ask the principal "Where have you been?"

To aid in the monitoring process, numeracy-focused assessment data, including standardized tests as well as other considerations such as samples of students' work, observations of students' in-class performance, and results of numeracy-based activities, benchmark exams, and projects should be collected and reviewed. In addition, it is helpful to look beyond formal assessment data to examine students' attitudes and gather comments from parents. Explore other sources of information that may give some insight into whether or not the goals of the numeracy program are being met, such as lesson plans and teacher notes, student and/or teacher self-evaluation surveys, classroom displays, informal discussions with teachers and students, and student participation in math-oriented cocurricular activities. During classroom visits, observers should note whether students appear to be confident, suitably challenged, and motivated learners of mathematics and if they are making appropriate progress in this area. These formative data give information to the numeracy team to gauge areas of success as well as areas needing adjustment.

Observation Hint: Student Learning

Try to answer these key questions:

- Do students engage readily in mathematical activities?

- Do students use vocabulary specific to the content area?

- Do students demonstrate the ability to think through and articulate solutions to mathematical challenges?

- Can students apply mathematical skills in a range of contexts?

- Do students use technology resources appropriately to support their learning?

The numeracy team reviews, analyzes, and presents all of the data collected, and makes recommendations regarding the value of various elements of the numeracy program and how well these elements further the success of students. As a result, the principal and the other observers may decide to make adjustments in areas in need of improvement. Because effective monitoring helps everyone gain a better understanding of the teaching–learning process, the groups must come to consensus early on regarding how the numeracy team will give feedback to the principal, leadership staff, and teachers regarding how well the evaluation of the numeracy program is being carried out.

Monitoring the numeracy program can yield great rewards:

- It leads to the implementation of the best teaching practices
- It provides opportunities for staff to reflect on current practices
- It helps the numeracy program to become integrated with the overall instructional program to support learning
- It helps to institutionalize the inquiry process in the school
- It provides information about students' progress from a variety of sources, including, but not limited to, standardized tests.

The process of monitoring is never really complete. During the final stages of a "cycle" (e.g., school year), teachers apply what they have learned and focus on actions provided through data collection and analysis that will most likely yield positive benefits for students. As teachers plan for the next cycle, they should be thinking in terms of short- and long-term goals. Their plans will be very specific, and you can assist by providing information on best teaching practices, up-to-date research, and the current thinking on how to directly improve students' numeracy skills. If you have involved your teachers in the ongoing planning, as well as the monitoring process, they will demonstrate "ownership" of the initiative and the importance of addressing mathematics skill areas specific to their classrooms. Changes will then be integrated into their daily lessons through enhanced instructional strategies. At this point, consideration also should be given to implementation of new curriculum, core courses, electives, and innovative methods of instruction. The new evaluation cycle will encompass tracking and monitoring the effectiveness of these newest ideas and actions, resulting in an ongoing cycle of continuous improvement. The ultimate payoff is that close monitoring of the school numeracy program will result in the implementation of better teaching practices in mathematics as well as the other content areas, opportunities for all teachers to reflect on current practices, improved instruction to support learning in all subjects, and, best of all, improved student performance in mathematics skills and problem solving.

Chapter 7:
Monitoring and Evaluating

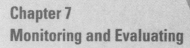

Commitment

_____ Establish an effective numeracy team to assist in ongoing monitoring efforts

_____ Share your commitment to directly observe the numeracy program implementation in each classroom with your faculty

_____ Communicate to your faculty the need for methods to track the progress of students, analyze the results of teaching methods, and discern the value of instructional materials used.

Monitoring

_____ Answer the question: What are we evaluating and why?

_____ Establish procedures to:

    _____ Collect relevant data on a periodic basis

    _____ Analyze and evaluate the information collected

    _____ Take action as a result to improve student performance

_____ Consider developing a classroom observation checklist

_____ Research the use of different types of principal monitoring:

    _____ Daily classroom visits

    _____ Walk-throughs

    _____ Formal evaluations with numeracy data collection form

_____ Collect and review numeracy-focused assessment data other than standardized test, such as:

    _____ Samples of students' work

    _____ Observations of students' in-class performance

    _____ Results of numeracy-based activities and projects

    _____ Students' attitudes

    _____ Parents' comments

    _____ Lesson plans and/or teacher notes

    _____ Teacher self-evaluation survey results

    _____ Classroom displays

    _____ Informal discussions with teachers

    _____ Informal discussions with students

    _____ Student participation in math-oriented cocurricular activities

_____ Set up procedures to create a monitoring cycle that:

    _____ Establishes purposes of monitoring and how it is related to achieving the Numeracy Improvement Plan goals

    _____ Assists teachers in applying what they have learned through data collection

    _____ Helps teachers, departments, and teams plan short- and long-term goals for the next cycle on the basis of an analysis of what will yield positive benefits for students.

Conclusion

Change the way you look at things…
You will change the things you see!

So where do you go from here? Change! Initiating a change will begin this process:

- **Change the culture around numeracy in your school.** A true test of a numeracy culture developing in your school means never hearing the following statements from your stakeholders:

Teacher:	Not everyone will be able to do algebra…
Student:	I was never too good at math…
Parent:	Math was never a strength in our family…
Counselor:	If you can just pass this course, you won't have to take math any more…
Counselor:	I'm scheduling you to Ms. Richardson so that you can pass this mathematics course required for graduation…
Principal:	I don't know why our math scores are going down…
Teams:	Just find the kids who are not doing well, pull them out, put them in a separate class, and…

  As long as your stakeholders continue to frame numeracy in these ways, you have not successfully created a culture of numeracy in your school.

- **Change the players.** Create collaborative teams for schoolwide implementation of the numeracy initiative and empower them to work. Involve community members and businesses in your team composition.

- **Change the way you use your teams.** A successful numeracy initiative needs collaborative teams to provide leadership for mentors, peer teachers, coaches, monitors, and evaluators.

- **Change the use of data.** If you don't test, then you don't know what to teach. Use the four types of data (perceptual, summative, formative, and demographic) to make your teachers and students data savvy and to create:
  - ❏ A School Numeracy Profile
  - ❏ A Personal Plan for Mathematics Proficiency
  - ❏ A Numeracy Improvement Plan.
- **Change what you teach and what you expect.** Raise the rigor in every classroom, selecting curriculum standards that emphasize depth of learning and reinforce mastery of mathematics skills across the content areas. Raise your expectations of every student, plan collaboratively and regularly by grade and department, and provide support for those students who need it.
- **Change the way you teach.** Utilize real experiences that connect the dots for students, assign activities that link problem solving with mathematics skills, use authentic assessments, give students the opportunity to plan collaboratively in the completion of projects, and support students toward mastery.
- **Change the way you prepare teachers.** Professional development should employ and model real-life examples; problem solving and differentiation strategies; faculty externships; continuing education (pedagogy, technology, instructional delivery) courses at the university, online, or in the community; and data-driven instruction.
- **Change the way you look at kids.** Raise expectations for all students, teach them to set learning goals based on personal data results, prepare them to accept the challenge of higher mathematics each year, and involve parents in the process.
- **Change the way you pay for things.** Explore learning grants, pilot programs, proposal writing, and partnerships for initiative funding.

Although the organizational aspects are crucial in creating the conditions for change, the core of all school change efforts are the beliefs, attitudes, practices, and characteristics that define the school's culture. These components of the organization can take longer and are often more difficult to change. School change is not necessarily a linear process, but can be best described as cyclical. Principals can expect to experience slow, steady progress, with occasional implementation dips as both initial and long-lasting changes take place over a specific period of time. While the principal must act as facilitator, coach, and supporter, it is fundamentally a team effort. Parents, community, students, educators must have a voice in the process.

So when thinking about implementation of new programs, management of change, not the proposed change itself, is one of the most important elements. It is widely accepted that key ingredients for successful change are a vision, skills, incentives, resources, and an action plan.

When any one of these components is missing, change becomes problematic. Each of the essential elements of planned change has certain requirements for success. For example, vision must be known and shared, with a clearly anticipated destination and specific reasons for the journey. If the principal is not able to articulate the vision effectively, there will be lack of clarity and support. Further, if the users do not possess the necessary skills, there will be anxiety and a lack of follow-though. Ensure that the skills required are taught and provide opportunities for guided collegial practice. If incentives are not present and valued by the stakeholders, there may be extremely slow (or no) change. The incentives for the change must be made explicit and the teacher must know how to use the new material and human resources for successful implementation. Moving from a shared vision to the action plan without identifying skills, incentives, and resources means that change, at best, will be tentative. Finally, the action plan must serve as the road map that utilizes all of the change components. A successful plan marks frequent milestones for progress as the school moves towards its numeracy goals.

As you take this journey on the path toward meeting numeracy goals for your school, remember that there is really no end or conclusion. This journey is actually a process that administrators, teachers, students, and parents move through every day. Great expectations, serious study, and daily practice certainly bring you closer, but numeracy is one of the lifelong journeys. To ensure that you stay on the path your school has chosen, continue to check and double-check your progress/change that you have planned for.

The principal makes decisions every day that affect the lives of the young people. No decision will make students more successful in life than those that encourage and assist them in taking sequentially challenging mathematics courses.

Conclusion

IN THEIR OWN VOICE ...

Woodbridge High School

Woodbridge High School is a small rural school in Bridgeville, DE, which decided to influence the academic achievement of its students by changing the culture of the entire school community. Led by a dedicated principal, the school staff devoted itself to changing the culture of the classroom, the school, and the community.

Since the inception of NCLB and AYP requirements, Woodbridge consistently ranked at or near the bottom of high schools in the state in academic achievement. At that time, Woodbridge had students, particularly in the 9th and 10th grades, who lacked a working knowledge of numeracy and did not have the skills necessary to perform basic operations and little foundation for higher math thinking or instruction. In addition, they had difficulty thinking through the process of solving mathematical problems logically and writing basic constructed responses as a means of understanding or solving math-related problems. The school also lacked the technology tools for teachers to effectively provide alternative and enhanced teaching strategies to differentiate instruction. With regard to test data, SAT scores were well below the national average in all categories, and the mathematics scores on the state test showed only one student in four achieving at a proficient or better level of competence. Under the Delaware accountability system, the school was in need of improvement with an overall Corrective Action rating in the Academic Progress classification. In the face of these challenges, Woodbridge instituted a process of culture change during the 2005 and 2006 school years. Principal Gary M. Rosenthal describes this journey:

> We began to move towards a course structure which was aligned with state curriculum standards and grade-level course expectations. We purchased SmartBoards and the latest TI calculators, Navigators, and software for each mathematics classroom and have provided professional development and training for all staff to support enhanced teaching strategies available through and as byproducts of this technology. We have also provided a variety of software applications for the staff to support their programs of instruction. We have placed Algebra I at the grade 9 level, and we provide differentiated course levels based on student need for additional support, ability, and the state testing levels [transferred to us] for the incoming grade 9 students. We not only offer double-dose math within our 9th and 10th grade academies, but also after-school Raider coaching and tutorial services provided to all athletes by the National Honor Society. We have added AP-level math courses as well as the Academic Challenge program at the local community college as vehicles to challenge and accommodate those students who elect them and are now able to achieve at higher levels. Finally, we have improved the intensity of our beginning-of-class warm-ups by not only using the information presented to assess prior knowledge but also parlaying that information into performance indictors throughout the lesson which follows.
>
> The most difficult issue facing our school community was to understand that students had to be challenged and that all students had to reach for or be pushed to a higher level. We came to the process conclusion, although not necessarily philosophical agreement, that students had to be met at their level of knowledge, understanding, and skill and had to be taken to greater heights. While that is something that our school improvement team as well as teachers continue to discuss, we have the new academy model in place at the 9th and 10th grade levels to facilitate this change. The other challenge was refocusing teacher philosophy

at the high school level with regard to literacy (in all subject areas, including math) from one of "reading and comprehending to learn" to one of "learning to read and comprehend." Our literacy coach, Sandy Switzer, provided opportunities and training for this shift of the school mindset and transformation to a culture of focused learning, as well as for a common language of teaching and learning to take hold in all of our classrooms.

Students rose to the challenge of the increased rigor, and there has been a gradual improvement in student self-esteem both as individuals and as students in a school that has long had a negative reputation in the area. It is also evident, and remarked upon by the Delaware secretary of education on a recent visit, that the school has taken on a "focused culture of learning" in the classrooms. We have evidence of a common language, in all subject areas, and all teachers are using a toolbox of "habits" which are designed to improve student understanding of instruction, textbooks and subsequent lessons. A new, easier methodology to solve word problems has been introduced in conjunction with a schoolwide numeracy focus on logic. In addition, students are not only asking and responding to higher-order questions but also developing strategies to increase their capacity and sustainability for learning. Finally, our students are proud to have the latest technology in place to support our numeracy initiative and to prepare them for the ever-changing world which is becoming increasingly more high-tech in terms of jobs, opportunities, and performance levels.

Two years ago (2005), 29% of Woodbridge students met the minimal level of proficiency in mathematics in the Delaware Student Testing Program; last year (2006), nearly 50% of the students tested proficient. As a result, the school moved from the bottom of the state rankings and for the first time reached AYP in mathematics.

Grade 10 DSTP Mathematics Results

Level	2001	2002	2003	2004	2005	2006
Level 1 Well Below the Standard	53.3	50	49.1	38	33.9	32.1
Level 2 Below the Standard	35.5	20.8	33.9	36	36.5	20.5
Level 3 Meets the Standard	9.3	20.8	11.6	20	25.2	37.5
Level 4 Exceeds the Standard	0	5.2	4.5	3	4.3	8.9
Level 5 Distinguished	1.9	3.1	0.9	3	0	0.9

SCHOOL FACTS
Woodbridge High School

LOCATION:
Bridgeville, DE

SCHOOL DISTRICT:
Woodbridge, DE

GRADE LEVELS:
9–12

POPULATION:
465

ECONOMICALLY DISADVANTAGED:
47.3%

RACIAL/ETHNIC GROUPS:
61.5% White
31.3% Black
7.1% Hispanic
0.2% Asian American

Conclusion

Appendix 1
Numeracy Capacity Survey

Download the template at www.principals.org.

> **Directions:**
>
> - Rate "Importance at Our School" for each item from 1 to 5.
> - Rate "Exists at Our School" for each item from 1 to 5.
> - Calculate the difference between column 1 and column 2.
> - When you have rated all items in both columns and recorded the difference in the third column, return the survey for compilation with those completed by other stakeholders at your school.

| 1 | 2 | 3 | 4 | 5 |

Importance rating: 1 = Not important; 5 = Very important

Practice Rating: 1 = Infrequent or rare occurrence at this school; 5 = Frequent or common practice at this school.

	Importance at Our School	Exists at Our School	Difference
Collaborative Leadership and School Capacity			
1. The principal's role in improving the school's numeracy opportunities is clearly evident.			
2. The principal and school leaders encourage collegial decision-making.			
3. The principal and school leaders support integration of numeracy instruction across the content areas.			
4. The principal, school leaders and staff members believe that numeracy is their responsibility.			
5. Adequate fiscal resources are provided to support numeracy.			
6. Data-driven decision-making guides numeracy improvement planning.			
7. Scheduling structures are in place to support the implementation of numeracy initiatives.			

	Importance at Our School	Exists at Our School	Difference
8. Scheduling structures are in place to support numeracy professional development.			
9. The school improvement plan includes numeracy as a major improvement goal.			
Strategic Use of Assessment			
10. School and student data sources are used to support the instructional improvement focus.			
11. Professional development to improve numeracy is based on assessment data.			
12. Standardized, formal assessments are used to assess the mathematics mastery of all students.			
13. Teachers utilize data to learn the numeracy capabilities of all students they teach.			
14. Assessment data is used in staff to plan and support student learning.			
15. The evaluation and monitoring process identifies skills mastered and not mastered by each student.			
16. Teachers use informal mathematics assessments within content classes to develop a better understanding of student numeracy instructional needs.			
Professional Development to Support Numeracy			
17. The numeracy team assesses and plans the numeracy professional development focus.			
18. Student numeracy needs drive professional development plans for teachers.			
19. Reflective teaching and self-assessment of instructional practices provide direction as to ongoing numeracy professional planning.			
20. Teachers with numeracy expertise and experience serve as models and mentors to less experienced colleagues.			
21. Data from informal/walkthrough visits provide areas of focus for numeracy professional development.			
22. Teachers participate in shared-teaching sessions to learn and refine numeracy strategies.			
23. Content area teachers receive ongoing, job-embedded professional development to learn instructional/numeracy strategies.			
Instructional Practices to Improve Student Achievement			
24. Content teachers use effective instructional activities in support of developing student numeracy.			
25. Teachers effectively use a variety of strategies to support numeracy.			
26. Teachers provide personalized support to each student based on assessed needs.			
27. Content teachers create numeracy-rich environments to support learning.			

	Importance at Our School	Exists at Our School	Difference
28. Content teachers effectively use small group instructional strategies to improve student numeracy.			
29. Teachers effectively use a variety of numeracy learning strategies for all students.			
30. Teachers effectively use a variety of numeracy strategies that support problem solving in the content area for all students.			
31. Teachers use technology to support improved numeracy for all students.			
32. Teachers regularly use vocabulary development strategies and formal numeracy language to support student learning.			
33. Teachers regularly use strategies to support the reading/mathematics connection.			

Intervention to Improve Student Achievement

	Importance at Our School	Exists at Our School	Difference
34. Administrators and teachers use assessment data to develop individual numeracy plans to meet the instructional needs of all students.			
35. Intervention is highly prescriptive and supports the identified numeracy deficits of individual students.			
36. Electives are available to support improved numeracy of struggling/striving students.			
37. Ample tutoring sessions are available to support improved student numeracy.			
38. The most highly skilled teachers work with both accelerated and struggling/striving students.			
39. Teachers effectively use numeracy strategies to support all students' learning of content.			
40. The school numeracy improvement Plan supports strategies ranging from intervention for struggling students to expanding the numeracy power of all students.			

Implementation Strategies

To compile planning information for your school, collect completed surveys from your staff and follow these instructions.

On each returned survey form in column 1 (importance at our school) find the number from 1 to 5 assigned to item 1.

Example: Column 1 ⬇

	Importance at Our School	Current Practice at Our School	Difference
The principal's role in improving the school's numeracy opportunities is clearly evident.	4		

Add the numbers placed in column 1 on each of the completed surveys and find the average by dividing the total by the number of respondents.

Example: Ten surveys with the numbers: 4, 3, 3, 2, 1, 3, 4, 5, 5, 4.

Add the numbers, and divide by the number of forms submitted: In this case, 34 ÷ 10 = **3.4**

Using a blank survey form, place the average for item 1 in column 1.

Column 1 ⬇

	Important to Our School's Numeracy Initiative	Current Practice at Our School	Difference
The principal's role in improving the school's numeracy opportunities is clearly evident.	3.4		

Continue in this manner for all items 1–41 for column 1.

Use the same method described in step 1 to compile the average survey results for the degree to which items 1–41 exist at your school. Record the averages in column 2.

Column 2 ⬇

	Important to Our School's Numeracy Initiative	Exists at Our School	Difference
The principal's role in improving the school's numeracy opportunities is clearly evident.	3.4	1.6	

Compute the difference between the importance rating (column 1) and the practice rating (column 2). Record the differences for Items 1–41 in column 3.

Column 3 ⬇

	Important to Our School's Numeracy Initiative	Current Practice at Our School	Difference
The principal's role in improving the school's numeracy opportunities is clearly evident.	3.4	1.6	1.8

NOW WHAT?

Using the survey results: Distribute and discuss the survey results in a faculty meeting, professional learning community gathering, or focus-group meeting.

STEP 1

Review the procedures used to compile information from the survey:

On this survey, numerical ratings of one through five have been given to each of the numeracy survey items in two categories:

How important do you think the items is to improving student achievement?
(1=not at all important; 5=very important)

To what degree is the item practiced in your school?
(1=not evident at all; 5=implemented and practiced to a high degree)

Explain that the ratings for each item were averaged across all respondents, and the difference between the importance rating and the practice rating was computed to arrive at the figure in the third column.

STEP 2

Organize participants into groups of five or six to complete the following activity. Read the directions for this activity.

1. Identify and discuss the areas where the difference between importance and practice are greatest and what the possible reasons might be.
2. Assume the role of school planning team members (teachers, parent, support staff) or technical consultants making recommendations to the principal of the school about issues needing immediate change. Using the results, along with other available data and school resources, help the "team" decide where to begin numeracy efforts. Be prepared to defend your advice.

STEP 3

Poll the group to determine results, and record the results on chart paper. Suggest that, depending on the situation, school leaders may want to begin with the areas where the largest amount of change is needed (because of a sense of urgency). Conversely, there may be times when the most effective tactic may be to begin in areas where they are assured of a number of "quick wins" or there is "low-hanging fruit" to motivate faculty members and gain momentum. You will also need to pay attention to instances where an unusually low level of importance is attached to an item.

STEP 4

Facilitate a brief discussion with participants about the results.

STEP 5

Submit results to the principal and numeracy team for consideration and action.

Appendix 2
Relationship Between Mathematics Courses Taken and Postsecondary Education and Workplace Financial Success

The following resources are available for principals and leadership teams to use in school and community meetings to bring a researched national perspective to numeracy discussions with stakeholders. These slides, integrated with local school data and mathematics perceptions, will help frame the urgency of increasing mathematics rigor in all content areas and supporting initiatives that bring a "culture of numeracy" to your school.

The PowerPoint slides, which may be accessed at the NASSP Web site, www.principals.org/numeracy, in conjunction with data slides from your school, may form the framework for your presentation.

Review the PowerPoint presentation at www.principals.org/numeracy.

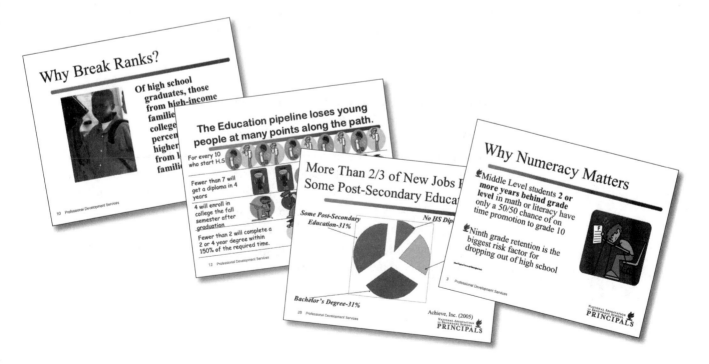

The research references are primarily from five sources and are all accessible on the Internet:

MetLife Survey of the American Teacher, 2003–2005
www.metlife.com (About Us > Corporate Citizenship > MetLife Foundation > Education)
This annual survey shows the vulnerability of new staff members and middle and high school students in transition to new schools (2005) and the discrepancy in the perception about school climate among school administrators, teachers, and parents (2003).

United States High School Sophomores: A Twenty-two Year Comparison, 1980–2002
http://nces.ed.gov/pubsearch/pubsinfo.asp?pubid=2006327
This report provides the original study and the results of two updates (1992 and 2002) on the *High School and Beyond Longitudinal Study* published in 1980 by the National Center for Education Statistics. The document presents information on the changing context of cohort demographics, family characteristics, school characteristics and school experiences, after-school activities, and future plans and expectations. Tested achievement is also presented with results in math from 1980 to 1990 and 2002, and results in reading from 1990 to 2002.

Math Matters: The Links Between High School Curriculum, College Graduation, and Earnings
www.pplc.org/content/pubs/report/R_701JBR.pdf
This study, conducted by researchers Heather Rose and Julian Betts, investigated the relationship of mathematics rigor and potential employment earnings. After flattening all variables of impact except the mathematics curriculum, a strong relationship was found between taking advanced math courses in high school and earnings 10 years after graduation.

Keeping Middle Grades Students on Track to Graduation
www.philaedfund.org
Liza Herzog, senior research associate at the Philadelphia Education Fund, and Robert Balfanz, associate research scientist at Johns Hopkins University, coauthored this study which followed sixth-grade students who attended Philadelphia public schools in 1996–97 through 2003–04 (a year beyond on-time graduation). They studied four high-risk factors that lead to dropping out of school: low attendance, poor behavior, and failure in mathematics and English courses. They also identified factors that can counteract student disengagement, such as whole-school reform, personalization, and individualized intervention.

ACT: Reading Between the Lines
www.act.org/path/policy/pdf/reading_report.pdf
This report is the result of a study of 1.2 million students who completed the ACT college entrance exam in 2005 and the impact of reading on grade level on English, mathematics, and science scores. It contends that while reading is now widely accepted as an interdisciplinary skill, so too must mathematics skills be seen as critical and applicable to all content areas.

Appendix 3
Begin the Conversation on Academic Rigor

The following activity begins the whole-school conversation about increasing academic rigor in all content classrooms. The exercise is timed so conversations can remain focused and moving. The activity outcome is to reach consensus on schoolwide and departmental definitions of academic rigor. The schoolwide definition is derived in approximately 25 minutes with added time for group discussion and debrief. The departmental definition may require 30–60 minutes of group discussion. Depending on the richness of the discussion, this activity can be accomplished in one or several sessions.

Begin this activity by saying:

We are going to use an activity to define a term that should have a schoolwide common and agreed-upon definition: academic rigor. Let's begin by reflecting on what we mean in this school when we say "academic rigor."

This activity can be used as you work with your faculty members or the broader community to illustrate the need for conversation and agreement about increasing academic rigor.

This is an individual and timed activity. You will need a sheet of paper. In the next two minutes, write your definition of "academic rigor."

Watch the time and at the end of two minutes announce:

Stop writing. Now, pair up with the person to your left. Combine your definitions so you have a written definition for "academic rigor" that both of you can live with.

Watch the time and at the end of three minutes announce:

Stop writing. Each pair should now take their definition and join another pair. You will now have four minutes to combine the two definitions. Remember that the result MUST be a written definition that all can live with.

Watch the time and after four minutes announce:

Stop writing. Each foursome should now take their definition and join with another foursome and, once again, discuss and combine your work into one written definition.

Group size will determine whether or not regrouping to form one definition is manageable. If the number of participants is manageable enough to regroup, discuss, and write one definition, ask a volunteer to write it on chart paper to share with the staff. Ask for a reader so all participants can listen carefully and reflect on the following elements as you hear the definition:

- Are all stakeholders included (e.g., students, parents, etc.)?
- Are the concepts and words in the definition understandable to a person without ties to the school?
- Are there major concepts or phrases that you wish had been included?

If the number in the writing groups has reached a size unmanageable for discussion and consensus (25 members or more), it may be difficult to continue this process until one definition is reached; therefore, you may want to stop the process and engage in a group discussion around the resulting three or four definitions that have been developed. Have a volunteer from each group write the group's definition on chart paper and hang it on the wall. Ask for a reader from each group. Ask all participants to listen carefully to each definition as it is read aloud. The participants will be asked to debrief the activity by identifying each of the following elements:

- What are the concepts, phrases, or words common to all the definitions?
- What are the major differences in the definitions?
- Are there concepts or phrases in one definition that you wish had been in your group's definition?
- Are the concepts and words in the definition understandable to a person without ties to the school?

Departmental Teams

Continue the discussion activity of defining "academic rigor" in departmental teams. Ask each department to meet, discuss the general definition(s) of "academic rigor" and the concepts and phrases in the final definition. Each department should craft a consensus definition in their content area: mathematics, language arts, physical education, etc. Introduce the idea of applying the "person on the street" standard to the understandability of each definition—in other words, you should expect the average person on the street to understand the definition. Discuss why understandability is crucial in communicating with members of the school community around reform efforts.

The result of this activity should be a rich discussion of academic rigor and content standards. Here are some points to infuse if they do not surface:

- Instruction includes high-level questions and thinking
- Teachers focus on what students know and are able to do
- Students create, develop, and publicly exhibit work
- All students are held to the same high standards
- Students and teachers use rubrics to evaluate work
- Teachers facilitate discussions
- All stakeholders understand the language used in the definition
- Students value the tasks assigned to them
- Students believe that they are capable of high-level work.

Each department should now put its definition into Practice. Probe teacher attitudes regarding the moral imperative as well as a federal mandate to educate all the children in the school's "subgroups" and discuss the **behaviors that are observed in a rigorous classroom**. Discussion-starters may include the following questions:

- What behaviors have you identified that tell you that the curriculum is rigorous?

- What are the behaviors that show high levels of student mastery?

- What are the behaviors that demonstrate skillful teaching?

- What are the behaviors that demonstrate engaged students?

Introduce the departmental activity with a consensus discussion on the observed teacher and student behaviors in a rigorous content class.

In the next few minutes in your departmental groups:

- *List five or more appropriate teacher behaviors that you would see in an academically rigorous middle level or high school classroom in your department.*

- *List five or more student behaviors that you would see in an academically rigorous classroom in your department.*

By consensus, finalize the departmental definition of academic rigor in your content area, list the observed teacher behaviors in these classrooms and list the observed student behaviors in these classrooms.

Make this information available to the numeracy team, administrative team, or the leadership team to assist in effective schoolwide monitoring and program evaluation.

This material is adapted from the Breaking Ranks II: Strategies for Leading High School Reform™ *and* Breaking Ranks in the Middle: Strategies for Leading Middle Level Reform™ *training modules.*

Appendix 4

Numeracy Across the Curriculum: Information-Gathering Template

Download the template at www.principals.org. Sample text is included below.

FOCUS AREA	DATA COLLECTION SOURCE	SUMMARY OF DATA COLLECTED	ACTION STEPS
STAFF VIEWS (Sample prompt: How do teachers see numeracy? How do they deal with numeracy in their content areas?)	EXAMPLES Survey, individual interviews, faculty meeting discussion notes, focus-group notes	EXAMPLES 43 of 50 content teachers do not use numeracy objectives for their classes	EXAMPLES ■ Undertake a curriculum review ■ Identify standards that support numeracy skills ■ Revise in the subject area curricula (i.e., language arts, social studies, art) ■ Develop interdisciplinary activities and instructional strategies to accompany newly created numeracy objectives
STUDENT VIEWS (Sample prompt: What do students think about using mathematics to help them in their school work and lives?)			
RESOURCES (Sample prompt: Do curricular and instructional resources have numeracy goals embedded?)			
APPLYING MATHEMATICS (Sample prompt: Is there evidence that students use mathematics to help them learn in other settings? Are links made between other content areas and mathematics?)			

FOCUS AREA	DATA COLLECTION SOURCE	SUMMARY OF DATA COLLECTED	ACTION STEPS
STUDENT PERFORMANCE (Sample prompt: In the content areas where numeracy objectives are apparent in the curriculum, is there evidence that students are mastering skills? If not, what problems are they having and how can you support concept mastery?)			
ASSESSMENT (Sample prompt: What conclusions can be drawn or judgments can be made about numeracy across the curriculum? Are students improving on benchmark and annual mathematics assessments?)			
ADDITIONAL FOCUS AREA			
ADDITIONAL FOCUS AREA			

Appendix 5
Numeracy Improvement
Action Plan Template

Download the template at www.principals.org/numeracy.

PRIORITY AREA:

DESCRIPTION: *(e.g., link to vision, student achievement, school data review)*

RATIONALE:

TARGETS:

    Short term:

    Long term:

ACTION:

    What *(describe actions)*:

    Who *(responsible individual(s))*:

    When *(set timelines)*:

        Quick wins: Moderately difficult undertakings: Difficult tasks:

RESOURCES:

    Human:

    Material:

    Staff development:

ALIGNED PROFESSIONAL DEVELOPMENT:

    Assessment to evaluate staff capacity and needs:

FUNDING CONSIDERATIONS:

    Budget (attach):

    Sources *(e.g., public, private, grants, etc.)*:

MONITORING CRITERIA:

Appendix 6
School Numeracy Profile Template

Download the template at www.principals.org/numeracy.

I. Perceptual Data

Summarize focus discussion data. Answer questions such as:

What student groups are proficient in mathematics? Why?

What student groups have not reached proficiency in mathematics? Why?

Should content teachers reinforce mathematics skills in the classroom?

II. Summative Data

Attach trend data (3–5 years) summarizing mathematics achievement by student group in tables, graphs, and charts. List attachments:

Summary of attached data:

What are you good at?

For purposes of instruction and initiative planning, list mathematics standards mastered by each student group.

What do you need to work on?

For purposes of instruction and initiative planning, list mathematics standards not mastered by each student group

III. Formative Data:

Attach tables, charts, or graphs detailing distribution and mastery by subgroup for benchmark exam results, final exam results, proficiency levels, mathematics grade point averages, etc.
List attachments:

Summary of attached data:

What are your student groups good at?

What do your student groups need to work on?

SAMPLE SUMMARY FORM:

Student Group:_____
(Complete columns as needed)

Mathematics Course	Percentage Enrolled	Final Exam Average	Math Final Grade Point	Average Benchmark Exam Score	Percentage Proficient or Above
Algebra					
Geometry					
Algebra II					
Advanced Algebra					
Calculus/AP					

IV. Demographic Data:

Attach tables, charts, or graphs that describe each student group's schoolwide attendance patterns, suspension trends, promotion and retention data, etc.

List attachments:

Summary of attached data:

What are the longitudinal demographic characteristics of:

Student groups who have achieved proficiency?
Student groups who have achieved advanced?
Student groups who have not achieved proficiency?

Appendix 7
Personal Plan for Mathematics Proficiency

Download the template at www.principals.org/numeracy.

Sample Personal Plan
For Mathematics Proficiency

STUDENT INFORMATION:

Student's name _____

Birth date_____ Grade_____

Address_____
Phone_____

PARENT/GUARDIAN INFORMATION:

Name(s) _____
Address_____

City _____

State _____ Zip _____

Home phone_____ Cell phone_____ E-mail_____

Final Observations/Interview Summary

Instructions: After reviewing the individual mastery profile and factual data with the student, summarize your findings and next steps (i.e., scheduling, support plans) below:

cc: guidance, student, parent

Part I: Perceptual Data

Instructions: The primary focus of student-staff interviews should be on attitudes and beliefs. Complete the chart below based on responses from the student to school-developed key questions. Students' attitudes about mathematics and perceptions regarding study habits should be included.

Key Question	Student Responses
Sample prompt: Are you good at mathematics? Why or why not?	
Sample prompt: In which mathematics courses have you experienced the most success? Describe your experiences.	
Sample prompt: In which mathematics courses have you had the least success? What makes you think that?	
Sample prompt: How many hours do you spend studying in your favorite subject and how many hours do you spend studying mathematics? Why?	
Sample prompt: Do you use mathematics skills in any other content class?	
School-developed key question	

Part II: Summative Data

Instructions: Complete the chart below using as many sources of standardized assessment data as possible.

Data Source	Results
Standardized mathematics test mastery profile	
Benchmark exam scores	
College entrance/Advanced Placement mathematics exam scores	
Other:	

Individual Mastery Profile

Areas of Mastery	Evidence of Attainment	Areas in Need of Work	Evidence of Attainment

Part III: Classroom Data

Data Source	Results
Previous marking period grades	
Unit test grades	
Exam grades	
Benchmark mathematics exam results	
Mathematics final exam grades	
Other	

Part IV: Demographic Data

Data Source	Results
Mathematics courses (note sequence)	
Grades	
Daily attendance record (absences) Class attendance record (absences) Tardy record (tardies)	
Discipline record and/or other	

Mastered Concepts	Evidence of Attainment

Nonmastered Concepts	Strategies	Evidence of Attainment

Appendix 8
Staff Professional Development Self-Assessment Survey

Download the template at www.principals.org/numeracy.

Rate the following topics to identify those that will be the most beneficial to you in your current assignment. (5=most beneficial, 1=least beneficial)

	5	4	3	2	1
1. Content/subject matter	O	O	O	O	O
2. Mathematics in the content area	O	O	O	O	O
3. Problem solving techniques	O	O	O	O	O
4. Effective teaching practices/projects, applications	O	O	O	O	O
5. Using technology in teaching	O	O	O	O	O
6. Differentiated instruction	O	O	O	O	O
7. Inclusion strategies/ELL, special ed, GT	O	O	O	O	O
8. Curriculum integration	O	O	O	O	O
9. Closing the achievement gap	O	O	O	O	O
10. Numeracy application strategies	O	O	O	O	O
11. Classroom management	O	O	O	O	O
12. Working in teams	O	O	O	O	O
13. Teachers as leaders	O	O	O	O	O
14. Peer coaching	O	O	O	O	O
15. Faculty externship	O	O	O	O	O
16. Conflict resolution	O	O	O	O	O
17. Mentoring and personalization	O	O	O	O	O
16. Behavior management	O	O	O	O	O
17. Parent communication/conferences, contacts	O	O	O	O	O
18. Family involvement strategies	O	O	O	O	O
19. Understanding and using data	O	O	O	O	O
20. Assessment	O	O	O	O	O

Appendix 9
Numeracy Budget Worksheet

Download the template at www.principals.org/numeracy.

School year: _____ Date: _____

Department/team:_____ Prepared by: _____

Directions:

List proposed departmental/grade-level team resources in support of the schoolwide numeracy plan.

Place all items in order of PRIORITY within categories; expand or add cells for additional information. Under Rationale, align the requests with specific initiatives. Think in terms of short- and long-term needs, using separate forms for each.

Equipment				
Rationale	**Item**	**Number**	**Cost/Item**	**Total**
			Subtotal	

Instructional Materials				
Rationale	Item	Number	Unit Cost	Total
			Subtotal	

Supplies				
Rationale	Item	Number	Unit Cost	Total
			Subtotal	

Facilities (including additions and modifications)				
Rationale	Facility	Number	Est. Value	Total
			Subtotal	

Services
(professional development, including on-site training and off-site externships, visits, etc.)

Rationale	Service	Number	Cost	Total
			Subtotal	

Travel
(including workshops, conferences, site visits, field trips)

Rationale	Item	Number	Cost	No. People	Total
			Subtotal		

Personnel

Rationale	Person	Salary	Benefits	Total
			Subtotal	

Numeracy Initiative Program Tool

Appendix 10
Observing for Numeracy Goals
in the Content Classroom

Download the template at www.principals.org/numeracy. Sample text is included below.

Numeracy Goals Observation Form

Date: _____

Teacher: _____ Subject: _____

Criteria are to be decided upon by departments/grade teams in cooperation with the administrative and instructional leaders. Areas to be considered may include climate, curriculum, instruction, technology, and assessment. The procedure may be similar to those used in walkthroughs or focus walks.

Criteria	Notes
Example: Does the teacher demonstrate the use of schoolwide accepted practice in: vocabulary, notations, conventions, labeling of graphs and charts?	
Example: Are opportunities presented for students to use and apply mathematics (i.e., problem solving, mathematics communication, reasoning)?	
Example: Do students show initiative and confidence in using instructional technology effectively to support their learning?	
Create school/department/team-specific criteria	
Create school/department/team-specific criteria	

References

Achieve Inc. (2006). *Closing the expectations gap 2006.* Washington, DC: Author.

ACT. (2006, August 16). *2006 national score report news release.* Retrieved December 30, 2006, from www.act.org/news/releases/2006/ndr.html

Arizona Department of Education. (2005–2006). Greatschools: Estrella Foothills High School. Retrieved: February 14, 2007, from www.greatschools.net/modperl/achievement/az/2746

Business–Higher Education Forum. (2006). *The American competitiveness initiative: Addressing the STEM teacher shortage and improving student academic readiness.* Issue Briefing. Retrieved November 18, 2006, from www.bhef.com/publications/issuebriefing3layout.pdf

Capital Area Institute for Mathematics and Science, Penn State. (n.d.). Services. Retrieved November 5, 2006, from http://mathscience.psu.edu/services/index.htm

Council for Corporate & School Partnerships. (n.d.). *A how-to guide for school-business partnerships.* Retrieved March 12, 2007, from www.corpschoolpartners.org/pdf/coke_how_to_guide.pdf

Delmore, P. (2000). Math makeover. *Principal Leadership*, 6(1), 40–42.

Education Trust. (2005). *Stalled in secondary: A look at student achievement since the No Child Left Behind Act.* Washington, DC: Author.

Farhi, P. (2007). Five myths about U.S. kids outclassed by the rest of the world. *Washingtonpost.com.* Retrieved January 29, 2007, from www.washingtonpost.com/wp-dyn/content/article/2007/01/19/AR2007011901360.html.

Feller, B. (2006, February 15). *Parents, students fine with math, science.* Associated Press. Retrieved December 16, 2006, from www.publicagenda.org/press/clips/rc06_clip_ap.pdf

Fulton, K., Burns, M., & Goldenberg, L. (2005). Teacher learning in networked communities: The TLINC strategy. *Phi Delta Kappan*, 87(4), 298–301.

Gainey, D. D., & Webb, L. D. (1998). *The education leader's role in change: How to proceed.* Reston, VA: NASSP.

Haycock, K. (2001, Winter). Actions for communities and states. *Thinking K–16*, 5(1), 18–22.

Haycock, K. (2002a, Summer). Add it up: Mathematics education in the U.S. does not compute. Thinking K–16, 6(1), 1–2

Haycock, K. (2002b, Summer). Still at risk. Thinking K–16, 6(1), 3–11, 14–23

Hopkins, G. (Ed.). (2006). Walk-throughs are on the move. *Education World.* Retrieved January 27, 2007, from www.education-world.com/a_admin/admin/admin405.shtml

Jerald, C. (2006, September). Using data: The math's not the hard part. *Issue Brief.* Washington, DC: Center for Comprehensive School Reform and Improvement.

Johnson, J., Arumi, A. M., Ott, A., & Remaley, M. (2006). *Reality check 2006: Are parents and students ready for more math and science?* Retrieved October 22, 2006, from www.publicagenda.org/research/research_reports_details.cfm?list=96

Kolata, G. (1997). Understanding the news. In L. A. Steen (Ed.), *Why numbers count: Quantitative literacy for tomorrow's America* (pp. 23–29). New York: The College Board.

Loucks-Horsley, S., Stiles, K., & Hewson, P. (1996). Principles of effective professional development for mathematics and science education: A synthesis of standards. *Teachers as Learners.* Madison, WI: National

Mero, D., Hartzman, M., & Boone, E. (2005). Building the future on knowledge. *Principal Leadership*, 5(10), 46–56.

Mirra, A. J. (2003). *Administrator's guide: How to support and improve mathematics education in your school.* Reston, VA: National Council of Teachers of Mathematics.

National Association of Secondary School Principals. (2004). *Breaking Ranks II: Strategies for leading high school reform.* Reston, VA: Author.

National Association of Secondary School Principals. (2005). *Creating a culture of literacy: A guide for middle and high school principals.* Reston, VA: Author.

National Association of Secondary School Principals. (2006). *Breaking Ranks in the Middle Leadership* training module. Reston, VA: Author.

National Council of Teachers of Mathematics. (n.d.). *Professional development of teachers of mathematics.* Retrieved October 22, 2006, from www.nctm.org/about/position_statements/position_statement_10htm

Owings, W. A., & Kaplan, L. S. (2004). School finance as investment in human capital. *NASSP Bulletin*, 88(640), 12–28.

Painter, B., Lucas, S., Wooderson, M., & Valentine, J. (2000). The use of teams in school improvement processes. Reston, VA: NASSP.

Perie, M., Grigg, W., & Dion, G. (2005). *The nation's report card: Mathematics 2005* (NCES 2006–453). U.S. Department of Education, National Center for Education Statistics. Washington, DC: U.S. Government Printing Office.

Public Agenda. (2006, Feb. 15). Reality check 2006: In case you haven't heard.... Press Release. Retrieved October 22, 2006, from www.publicagenda.org/press/pdfs/rc06-quotes.pdf

Rose, H., & Betts, J. (2001). *Math matters: The links between high school curriculum, college graduation, and earnings.* San Diego, CA: Public Policy Institute of California. Retrieved December 15, 2006, from www.pplc.org/content/pubs/report/R_701JBR.pdf

Schmoker, M. (2001). *The results fieldbook: Practical strategies from dramatically improved schools.* Alexandria, VA: Association for Supervision and Curriculum Development.

Sparks, D. (2001). NSDC revises staff development standards. National Staff Development Council. Retrieved October 22, 2006, from www.nsdc.org/library/publications/results/res5-01spar.cfm

Sterling, D. R. (2004). The teacher shortage: National trends for science and mathematics teachers. *Journal of Mathematics and Science: Collaborative Explorations, 7,* 85–96.

Wagner, T., & Kegan, R. (2006). *Change leadership.* San Francisco, CA: Jossey-Bass.

Weiss, I. (2006). *Issues in designing professional development for teachers of mathematics.* Horizon Research, Inc. Retrieved March 11, 2007, from www.horizon-research.com/presentations/2006/ncsm_april06.pdf

Yergalonis, E. (2005). A principal's journey. *Principal Leadership*, 6(4), 40–43.